CYBERCRIME
AND THE DARKNET

INTRODUCTION

In 2016, a phenomenal leak of 11.5 million records from Mossack Fonseca, a law company based in Panama, exposed to the world the hidden financial exploits of some of the wealthiest individuals on the planet. The disclosure illustrates how law companies and banks sell financial secrecy indiscriminately to the wealthy – whether they be politicians, billionaires, celebrities, fraudsters or drug traffickers – by setting up tax havens in which they can keep all their transactions hidden. Although already possessing untold riches, clients of such outfits use their services to hide corrupt practices from the prying eyes of the authorities and evade the taxes that the rest of us have to pay.

The release of the Panama Papers was the culmination of an extraordinarily detailed investigation by the International Consortium of Investigative Journalists, the German newspaper *Süddeutsche Zeitung* and more than 100 other news organizations. In the largest media collaboration ever, more than 370 reporters pored over millions of Mossack

A folder displaying the Mossack Fonseca logo and containing US and EU currency together with a flash drive that holds some of the Panama Papers.

Fonseca's documents disclosed to them by whistleblowers and shared their findings.

Among those exposed were 12 current and former world leaders, including China's leader Xi Jinping, who in his official capacity had led anti-corruption efforts. The prime minister of Iceland, Sigmundur David Gunnlaugsson, was shown to be a secret multimillionaire, stashing his fortune in a secret offshore company that kept millions of dollars in Icelandic banks. Following the revelations, he was forced to resign. A total of US $2 billion worth of transactions were revealed to be linked to the Russian president Vladimir Putin. In the UK, the prime minister at the time, David Cameron, admitted that he had benefited from an offshore trust set up in Panama by his late father.[1]

How did Mossack Fonseca do it? The firm worked with more than 14,000 banks and law companies to set up trusts and fake companies, known as shell structures, for its customers, where they could hide their assets. Paper and electronic records of transactions were destroyed so they could not be traced. These activities may be considered unethical but they are not illegal if used by law-abiding citizens.

Ironically, it is the whistleblowers who reveal such confidential documents who are considered cybercriminals. To access and expose those materials, they operate on the Darknet, using illicit hacking techniques and untraceable communications. Are those who carry out such actions lawless hackers, guilty of releasing millions of secret documents that should never see the light of day? Or are they committed but misunderstood activists, devoted to exposing the corruption and abuse of power of powerful people through freedom of information? This is just one of the conundrums of cybercrime and the Darknet.

DEFINING CYBERCRIME AND THE DARKNET

It's worth trying to unpick exactly what these terms mean. Cybercrime is any use of a computer for illegal reasons, including fraud, identity theft, stealing intellectual property, violating privacy or sharing child sexual abuse images. Cybercriminals frequently hack into computer systems, although they also use social engineering – persuading people to reveal private information that allows fraudsters to access their data. Many cybercriminals operate for financial gain, but others act to expose corruption or for political motives. The latter use illegal means but claim their reasons are legitimate.

Hackers

Hackers are labelled white-, grey- or black-hat according to the shades of legality and legitimacy of their actions. Hacktivists are hackers who infiltrate sites and expose information for political purposes. White- and grey-hat hackers and hacktivists believe they act legitimately.

- White-hat hackers look for information or simply enjoy the challenge of breaking into systems to expose their vulnerabilities. Security companies, governments and big businesses employ white-hat hackers to protect their sites.

- Grey-hat hackers are prepared to break the law to find and publicize security vulnerabilities.[2]

- Black-hat hackers, also known as 'crackers', steal data and seize control of websites to commit fraud.

All hackers operate by looking for weaknesses in a computer network security system, using 'packet sniffers' – software that searches for information being passed along computer networks, including passwords. Hackers call firewalls 'cotton walls' because they tend to have weaknesses that allow intruders to penetrate them easily.

You don't have to be a hacker to be a cybercriminal. It's easy to purchase hacking services or stolen data on the Darknet.

The Darknet

The Darknet is part of the Deep Web, the biggest part of the Internet, which is not indexed by regular search engines. It's where public databases are found, along with subscription-only and password-protected services, and the content of social networks and messaging sites. The Darknet can be accessed via the Tor browser, and Tor Hidden Services allow you to find anonymously run websites. No one uses his or her real name on the Darknet.

Neither cybercrime nor the Darknet are straightforward – they are a morass of contradictions and grey areas. Cybercriminal activity occurs on the surface net: harassment, copyright infringement, fraud, subversion, sabotage and terrorist propaganda. But although these actions are illegal, are some of them legitimate? Those who believe information should be free oppose copyright laws, while cybersubversion and cybersabotage can help topple authoritarian regimes; they were vital catalysts in the 2010–11 Arab uprisings.

Cybercrime is big on the Darknet, too: witness the vibrant trade in illegal goods and services, proliferation of child sexual abuse and organization of terrorist actions. Cryptocurrencies such as Bitcoin and blockchain technology developed on the Darknet to enable anonymous payments to be made. But is it possible to identify legitimate elements here, too? Cryptocurrencies are used for lawful as well as illicit trade, and some argue that the drugs market is safer on the Darknet than on the streets. And while governments consider whistleblowing that reveals state secrets to be a crime, freedom of information activists consider it a duty. On the Darknet, human-rights and political activists enjoy privacy, a safe haven where they can avoid surveillance. Creativity blossoms in an atmosphere free from censorship and commercial advertising.

SURVEILLANCE

Mass surveillance is a major reason that both cybercriminals and privacy activists have shifted to the Darknet. Governments and security companies are monitoring every aspect of our online lives. On both the surface net and Darknet, they adopt similar tools to the cybercriminals to fight them, using Trojans (see page 34) to hack into their systems and posing as fellow-fraudsters to ensnare outlaws and bring them to justice. Governments carry out cyberespionage and sabotage operations, arguing that their actions are justified to protect people from terrorism and child sexual abuse. However, some people believe that governments overstep the mark and abuse their power.

Cybercrime and the Darknet is divided into two sections. Section 1 focuses on cybercrime. Chapter 1 considers serious online harassment that has been defined as illegal, from cyberbullying to trolling, doxing and grooming, and whether the law can tackle such abuse. Chapter 2 looks at the wide variety of online fraud we risk as individuals – from email scams, malware and phishing to identity theft – and big-business heists including cyberattacks on banks and corporations. Chapter 3 examines how copyright laws are pitched against freedom of information activists and asks whether there can be a happy medium that enables the creators of music, books and movies to make a living while allowing free access to their products.

Chapter 4 surveys the range of online subversion, from individual jailbreaking of devices to hacking to expose corruption and abuse, and mass political activism as a prelude to real-world uprisings. It illustrates how governments attempt to clamp down on these activities using entrapment and heavy penalties for offenders. Chapter 5 considers the rising threat of cyberattacks: cyberespionage for information gathering; cybersabotage, from the defacing of a website to damaging infrastructure; and cyberterrorism, focusing on the online coordination of terrorist actions by the so-called Islamic State (ISIS).

Section 2 is about the Darknet. Chapter 6 enters the hidden world of dark markets, where all manner of illicit goods and services are traded. Drugs are the most popular – Ross Ulbricht's Silk Road (2011–13) set the standard for the trade, adopting Bitcoin for transactions – while there has been an explosion of child sexual abuse sites. The efforts to shut down illegal markets are explored. Chapter 7 investigates the Darknet as a place of privacy and anonymity for human rights, political and freedom of information activists, of cryptocurrencies for the unbanked and creativity for musicians. It raises the question: can governments balance their desire for mass surveillance for national security and law enforcement with privacy and civil liberties for individuals?

CYBERCRIME

CHAPTER 1

HARASSMENT:
Cyberbullies, Trolls, Doxers and Groomers

It's hard to know who you're talking to on the Internet; people often invent a new persona for themselves – someone of a different age, gender or country of origin. And people behave differently online from how they do in real life. Face to face, people monitor the reactions of others around them and modify their behaviour accordingly. Body language, facial expressions and eye contact all give us signals as to what the other person is thinking and feeling, and all of these are lacking online unless video links are used. Many sites are used anonymously, giving people the liberty to develop a variety of alternative identities.

This freedom can be positive – online, people may be more open or honest and able to discuss issues or problems they cannot express in person. But it is sometimes negative, allowing them to be abusive towards other Internet users. Discussions that begin in a reasonable manner may rapidly grow more aggressive and nasty; chat between potential partners becomes intimate too quickly. Sites that are moderated are more polite because offensive comments are not tolerated, but where anything goes, insults may reign.

Suler's Online Disinhibition Effect is often used to explain how online interactions can so readily escalate into harassment. In 2004, psychologist John Suler identified six factors that change people's behaviour online:

1. 'DISSOCIATIVE ANONYMITY' – no one can attribute my actions to me

2. 'INVISIBILITY' – nobody knows what I look like

3. 'ASYNCHRONICITY' – my actions are not happening in real time

4. 'SOLIPSISTIC INTROJECTION' – I cannot see other people, so I guess who they are and what they want

5. 'DISSOCIATIVE IMAGINATION' – because this is not the real world, these are not real people

6. 'MINIMIZING AUTHORITY' – I can do what I want because no one is in charge.[3]

These factors make it incredibly easy for harassment to take place on the Internet. At the mildest levels, online pestering can be unpleasant but not illegal. Where is the line between annoying but not illicit content and criminal activity? When do cyberbullying and stalking slip into cybercrime? How do you judge when the trolls and pranksters have gone too far? Some activities clearly cross the line into illegal content: it's clear that adults grooming children with a view to abusing them is a crime. Laws are continually being developed to criminalize harassment, but treating it as cybercrime may not necessarily be the most successful approach. In the long term, perhaps, protecting our identities more carefully and using social control to discourage unacceptable behaviour could prove more effective.

CYBERBULLYING AND STALKING

A 2015 survey in UK schools showed that traditional forms of bullying were still more common than online bullying.[4] Yet 11 per cent of children had endured cyberbullying and it was more common among girls (15 per cent) than boys (7 per cent). At its lowest level, unpleasant but not illegal harassment includes sending rude and offensive messages, untrue and damaging information about others or altering photos and posting them online. Also not necessarily illegal are flaming – using extreme and offensive language to cause arguments and distress to others, and social engineering – tricking people into revealing personal information or incriminating photos to use against them.[5]

Cyberstalking is the targeting of an individual for harassment, repeatedly sending intimidating messages threatening to harm them and making them afraid for their safety. Making threats on the Internet is a criminal offence and anyone who experiences it should make a complaint to the police.

CASE STUDY: BULLIED TO DEATH

Australian Jessica Cleland, 19, took her own life after merciless bullying by two teenage boys who said they hated her. On Facebook, she was bombarded with nasty messages, including being called a 'f***ing sook' (someone who whines or is overly sensitive)[6] and told that 'she should just get over things'. The bullies continued: 'if you come around to my place, I'm going to slam the door in your face. You're useless.'[7]

Eleven per cent of school children have endured cyberbullying and, while not illegal, it is often very harmful to the individuals involved.

Before the bullying, Jess was a happy young woman with no signs of mental health issues and was looking forward to her gap year. Yet when two former friends began to abuse her on Facebook and Snapchat, she became withdrawn, not even confiding in her sister Amy. At 7.30 a.m. on Easter Saturday, April 2014, Jess sent a text to her parents saying she was going for a run on the property next to theirs. When she hadn't returned a few hours later and didn't answer her phone, her worried parents went to look for her. Amy noticed that Jess had posted a picture on Instagram captioned 'I love this place and I am never going to leave.'[8] At the spot where she'd taken the photo, her father Michael found Jess's body, already cold.

Unable to understand what had gone so disastrously wrong, Jess's parents checked her iPad. They found 87 hurtful messages had been posted to her in just an hour and a half. She had pleaded with her attackers to stop but they had just kept going. The family had no idea things had gone so badly wrong.[9] The Clelands felt let down by police officers, who failed to take Jess's devices for examination in order to investigate this online harassment. The officers could have used a warrant to make Snapchat and Facebook reveal all communications, including deleted messages. They didn't even question the two bullies who had been attacking Jess so viciously. In her report into the death, coroner Jacqui Hawkins said that Facebook and text messaging 'were problematic for Jessica because easy access to the Internet on her phone meant that she was exposed to potentially upsetting communications 24 hours a day.'

Mrs Cleland commented, 'If you accidentally hit someone in your car you can get manslaughter. What's the difference if you bully someone and cause them to take their own life?'[10]

The Clelands and other parents of children who had killed themselves because of cyberbullying set up a group to try to prevent further suicides, and Michael Cleland signed up to be an ambassador with the Bully Zero Australia Foundation. Some parents say their children should give up social media but Michael disagrees: 'Why should they, just because someone else is misusing it? It's their connection to the outside world.'[11] He believes the onus should be on stopping the abusers, whether through the police or a sea-change in social attitudes that makes such behaviour as unacceptable in cyberspace as it would be face to face.

IMPERSONATION

Impersonation can be relatively innocent – we've all heard of children who find a parent's Facebook page open on the computer and post a silly message to their friends. This isn't hacking – the page was already open. But deliberately hacking into someone else's account and impersonating them to send out nasty messages or embarrassing information crosses the line into illegal territory.

TROLLS AND PRANKSTERS

Leo Trayner was targeted for three years by a vicious troll on Twitter. One day, he gained a new follower, followed back and then an abusive DM (direct message) arrived: 'Dirty F**king Jewish scumbag'. He blocked and reported the sender. The same thing kept happening. Then Traynor's Facebook and email accounts were hacked and flooded with foul messages relating to the Holocaust. One day, a parcel arrived at his home address containing a lunchbox full of ashes and a message saying 'Say hello to your relatives from Auschwitz.' The troll followed up with death threats. Petrified, Traynor closed his social media accounts and sought help from an IT-savvy friend, who identified three IP addresses used by the troll. He was shocked to find one linked to the 17-year-old son of a friend. When confronted face to face, the teenager claimed 'It was like a game' – and finally offered Traynor a heartfelt apology.[12]

The web has become a playground for pranksters and trolls, many of whom hang around 4chan. Set up in 2003 by Christopher Poole when he was 14, 4chan is an image-sharing site that allows people to post what they like, completely anonymously. Poole's aim was to carve out a separate part of the Internet away from big business, the authorities and ordinary users. There are forums for a million and one topics, but the random /b/ forum, where absolutely anything goes, has become a favourite haunt for trolls. The catchphrase 'I did it for the lulz' is invoked to justify any prank carried out for a laugh at someone else's expense, from offensive comments to downright illegal activities such as releasing people's confidential information (see page 23). Trolls range from bored, entertainment-seeking teens to serious libertarians with a political agenda.[13]

Trolls go to extremes. They will laugh at anyone for anything, even joking about a young person's suicide by posting insults on their Facebook page. To evade detection, they hide away, using proxy servers to mask their IP addresses (proxy servers allow you to make indirect connections to other network servers through an intermediary) and having many accounts under different pseudonyms or nicknames. If they get banned from a forum, they simply join under a new name. Trolls often coordinate attacks from secret channels and chat rooms and spar among themselves to sharpen their wits.

Notorious troll weev (Andrew Auernheimer) is a former president of an exclusive trolling clique, with the offensive name Gay Nigger Association of America (GNAA). In 2010 he discovered that US telecommunications company AT&T had put its customers' iPad data on the Internet unencrypted. Goatse Security, the GNAA's security group, found out how to 'slurp' the data (read entire data files) very easily. The group exposed this lack of security by going straight to the media. In November 2012 weev was convicted of hacking (although his group had not actually hacked the data because there was no security to break through) and sent to jail, where he remained until April 2014. Arguably, weev had shown responsibility by revealing the security breach; the security industry relies on hackers to discover vulnerabilities in computer systems so they can be fixed. He also did it for the lulz – knowing that when people Googled Goatse Security they would see one of the Internet's most revolting images of a hunched man pulling apart his butt cheeks freakishly wide.

On the other hand, weev has been called a 'menace on the Internet', with views that are abhorrent to most. He calls himself a 'defender of Western civilization', opposes multiculturalism and fears the spread of Sharia law in the West. His trolling activities include posting racist speeches against Jews and African-Americans on YouTube.[14] weev believes trolling is good for destroying the narrative of the opposition and upholding 'European virtues'.[15]

Other trolls have libertarian ideas. Named 'Britain's vilest troll' by British tabloid newspaper the *Daily Mail* in 2013, Old Holborn is known for his vitriolic online abuse of the families of the 96 people who died in the Hillsborough football stadium disaster of 1989. He believed that the Hillsborough families suffered from victimhood – they enjoyed being victims – and that he was exposing hypocrisy.[16] To him, pushing the boundaries forces people to be tough. If they are easily offended, there will be self-censorship, which affects freedom of speech. If you want a free society, then it should be possible to challenge or ridicule everything. But to many people, harassing the bereaved relatives of accident victims and causing them psychological damage is a giant step too far.

'THERE ARE NO GIRLS ON THE INTERNET' (RULES OF THE INTERNET, NO. 30)

Far fewer women than men post on image boards such as /b/ – although a surprisingly large number are transgender. There are some infamous female trolls, including Mercedes Haefer, who joined Anonymous in 2010, aged 19, and was convicted for the Distributed Denial of Service (DDoS) attacks on PayPal (see page 81).

DOXERS

Doxing is discovering an anonymous poster's real identity and using it to shame them in public as a prank or for a political motive. It has developed into a fine art. Some doxers use hacking or deception to gain access to information, but others manage to use publicly available data – even if their victim is using a pseudonym. They look for anything that might indicate the target's physical location, using big-data tools – for example, checking if they are likely to tweet about a certain place to work out where they are. Then they can look at public records for that area. Doxers also check out

Anita Sarkeesian in 2013: the online attacks against her continued after she spoke out against misogyny in video games. Women are far more likely to suffer serious harassment online than men.

different social media sites. Many people have multiple accounts linked together, so they can do a search on a site for all that person's postings or put the name into Google, and cross-reference between the different sites. They can also get data from illegal hacked sources. Sometimes, doxers go through the person's ISP, if they can locate it – there are ways of fooling ISP staff to access data about the account behind the IP address.[17] Well-known public figures appear not to be above doxing their rivals; in 2015, US presidential candidate Donald Trump doxed his opponent Senator Lindsey Graham by giving out his mobile number in public.[18]

Doxing can be used as a weapon in online arguments. In the Gamergate dispute of 2014, a few women complained about sexism in video games, and some game enthusiasts responded by doxing the critics, sharing personal information about the women who spoke out. Feminist commentator Anita Sarkeesian, game developer Brianna Wu and actress Felicia Day received rape or death threats. Wu recalled, 'I was literally watching the chat room as the site posted my address and the conversation moved to places that threatened my personal safety.' Fearing attack, she was forced to leave her home.[19]

Doxing per se may not always be illegal.[20] But laws against cyberstalking, harassment and threatening behaviour cover incidents such as the Gamergate revelations. Releasing confidential data such as an individual's social security or PIN number is certainly unlawful.[21] However, even if the culprit is caught, the material is still out there in cyberspace. Cleaning up after a doxing operation is tricky; victims can use the Digital Millennium Copyright Act (DMCA) to get photos taken down, but it can be hard work to make it happen.

GROOMING

Online grooming is definitely illegal territory. Paedophiles often befriend their victims in chat rooms. The chat can become sexual incredibly quickly, with the groomers then arranging to meet the victim: chat logs reveal that this process can take just 18 minutes.[22] Online grooming has made it far easier for paedophiles to get to know children and start talking about sex. The UK Child Exploitation and Online Protection Centre (CEOP) has noted an increase in purely online abuse,[23] while the charity Childline reported in December 2015 that online grooming cases had increased by nearly 50 per cent in the previous year.[24] Online groomers typically target girls aged 13 to 15. According to the *Journal of Adolescent Health,* the majority of sex crimes against children start in chat rooms.[25]

Groomers are extremely skilled at getting information out of their victim through what appears to be harmless chat. This extract from a chat log was part of the evidence used by Italian police to convict a 47-year-old groomer who went on to abuse children, and shows how he extracted information from a 13-year-old.

(G = GROOMER; V = VICTIM)

G: I wish you a happy Easter!

V: Tell me who r u?

*G: My name's A***** what's your name?*

*V: L****, what's your surname?*

G: Why do you want to know my surname, you don't know me?

V: Just curious. How old are you?

G: 20 and you?

> *V: 13 but my cell number? Who gave it to you?*
> *G: No one, I must have mistaken the number I though[t]*
> *it was my friend's sorry. Am I not too old for you?*
> *V: ok ok ... I don't think so.*
> *G: Do you mind if we know each other better, here in*
> *the chat line? ... Are you already tired of writing to me*
> *in chat? ... what are you doing?*[26]

It is not only the groomers whose tactics have grown increasingly sophisticated. The growing sexualization of children means it is sometimes the child who opens up the sexual phase in an online relationship.[27] Young people may also retaliate against online groomers, deliberately trying to 'bag a paedo' for fun. They entice the paedophile until he or she has revealed sufficient information for the young person to threaten to contact the police.

Yet although there has been an explosion in online grooming activity and there is far more contact between paedophiles and children online than there was 20 years ago, there is no clear evidence of an increase in recorded physical abuse.[28] Just as before the spread of the Internet, most young people who endure abuse suffer at the hands of someone they know, such as a relative or family friend.

BEATING THE BULLIES AND PAEDOPHILES

Governments are running to keep up with the challenges of cyberbullying, trolling and grooming. In Australia, the Enhancing Online Safety for Children Act 2015 appointed a Children's e-Safety Commissioner, responsible for administering a complaints system for cyberbullying material aimed at Australian children and making sure it is rapidly removed from social media sites.[29] A new law against trolling was passed in

New Zealand the same year, banning 'harmful digital communications', with a penalty of up to two years in prison. However, critics accused the definition of 'harmful' as being too broad, and having the potential to impede free speech.[30]

In some countries, law enforcers use entrapment to lure paedophiles and expose them. In one case in Australia in 2015, a 36-year-old schoolteacher from New South Wales thought he had found a 13-year-old girl to befriend in an online chat room. Over the weeks, he started to make sexually explicit comments and encouraged the girl to meet him. At 8.30 one morning, the teacher was arrested and charged with transmitting indecent communications and attempting to procure a child under 16 for sexual activity. Detectives from the sex crimes squad had posed as the girl to ensnare him.[31]

Although laws and the actions of sex crimes units clearly have their place, they alone cannot provide sufficient protection online. Personal security is key. Young people are starting to protect themselves by using fake personas or nicknames and only revealing their true identity to a small circle of real-life friends to reduce the likelihood of grooming and harassment. A change in our constantly evolving Internet culture could make a huge difference. Trolls want a reaction. If people refuse to 'feed the trolls' and instead develop a thick skin and learn to ignore deliberately provocative comments, then trolling might stop. If it becomes as socially unacceptable to harass people online as it is offline, then it could become less common.[32] Groups may turn on the offender straight away, ostracizing them from the conversation so that they will think twice about continuing their insults. As social policing on the Internet develops it is possible that these inter-personal crimes will decline.

CHAPTER 2

HITTING YOUR WALLET:
Internet Fraud

One Friday evening, Mr Tewari of Navimumbai in Maharashtra, India, received an SMS from his bank stating that he was about to receive a payment through Internet banking and was asked to log in to his account, entering the verification code provided. Not aware that he was about to receive a payment, he ignored it. The following morning, he received another message saying that his details had been received – even though he hadn't responded to the text. Twenty-four hours later, Mr Tewari discovered that 4 lac 60 thousand rupees (US $6,881/£4,715) had been taken out of his account. Mr Tewari called the police.

Online bank fraud is notoriously hard to solve. How could the police find the perpetrator? The hacker could have cracked Mr Tewari's Internet banking password through sending a phishing email or perhaps placed a keylogger on his PC to record his bank login details as he typed them in. Or maybe his mobile SIM card had been cloned to access his details. To find the cybercriminals, the police needed to find out who had added Mr Tewari as a beneficiary for the supposed payment through his bank account. From which IP address had it been requested? Who confirmed his details on Mr Tewari's behalf? Since the hacker had done this via an SMS, it appeared likely that the hacker had cloned the victim's SIM card. Which account did the money go into, and where were the funds withdrawn?

The police searched for the server that had sent out the SMS, using IP tracing tools such as 'what is my IP.com', and traced the IP address to a Hong Kong TV company. But the hacker had probably used an anonymizer to disguise the true IP address. Police investigators succeeded in locating the beneficiary bank account – Standard Chartered Bank, Lucknow, Uttar Pradesh (UP) branch. Checking with the mobile service provider, they discovered that five phone numbers with different addresses and identities were linked to that account. They then found the IP address of the device that was used to transfer the funds – a mobile used in Agra Railway station. Now they had to check all five numbers, addresses and identities to find the correct person. They examined CCTV footage of the Standard Chartered ATM to identify the fraudster who withdrew the money. The police placed this suspect under surveillance. As luck would have it, he bought jewellery worth 1 lac 90,000 rupees (US$2,842/ £1,948) from a shop in Allahabad, UP – bingo! Using the bank ATM and jewellery-shop CCTV footage and the suspect's ID photo, the police finally had the evidence to arrest him.[33]

Internet fraud incidents such as this occur daily around the world. The problem is growing at a disturbing rate and costing online companies and customers billions of dollars each year. It's been estimated that businesses alone lose US $400 billion (£275 billion) a year through cyberattacks.[34]

Customers are targeted by email through scams, malware and phishing attacks, and may have their identity stolen online. Despite tough security, banks fall prey to major hacks and their customers are hit by 'carding' – the fraudulent extraction of cash through ATMs; fake online businesses abound; and cybercriminals target legitimate businesses from the inside and the outside. Security companies and law enforcers fight back with anti-fraud protection systems, mass surveillance of online activity and tough legislation. But can they ever beat the cybercriminals?

EMAIL SCAMS, MALWARE AND PHISHING

User negligence can open the door to fraud. Creating, entering and changing secure passwords takes time, so security is a drain on productivity. Cormac Herley, a security researcher at Microsoft Research in Redmond, Washington, United States estimated that Internet users around the world spend the equivalent of 1,389 years every day entering passwords.[35] To avoid the effort, people tend to use simple, easy-to-guess passwords: according to CBT Nuggets, the most frequent words used in passwords in 2016 were 'love', 'star', 'girl' and 'angel'; also common were 'Mike' and 'John'[36]. People often have passwords to do with their lives, such as the name of their pet or a number from their date of birth. These are easy to guess for anyone who has access to publicly available basic information about them. It remains common to use the same password for all accounts. When people are forced to create complicated passwords, they often write them down in an accessible place near their desk at work. Alternatively, they may not bother to work in a secure network because it runs slowly.

All these factors make it relatively easy for a hacker to get lucky and break into somebody's account. Then they can send out emails to everyone in the victim's address book. Most people will have received emails of this nature:

'I'm writing this with tears in my eyes, I and my family [are] presently on a short trip to Istanbul, Turkey. Unfortunately, I was robbed in the hotel I booked, all my valuables which includes cash, mobile phones were stolen during the attack but luckily I still have my passport with me. I've been to the Embassy and the Police here but they are not taking the matter seriously. Please, I really need your financial assistance now because things are really getting tough on me here. Our flight leaves in few hours from now but we're having problems settling the hotel bills and the hotel manager won't let us leave until we settle the bills. Please, let me know if you can help us out? I'll really appreciate your prompt response. Regards . . .'[37]

This kind of scam has been around for several years, although nowadays the emails tend to be better written and more plausible than they used to be. A friend of this author lives in a small village and is a frequent traveller. Her email account was hacked and used to send a believable SOS message to all her contacts saying she was stranded without funds in Scandinavia. One Danish friend was excited to think he might be able to help her in person. Several neighbours got in touch by phone offering money to help out. One even responded to the email and tried to send her funds online but grew suspicious when the replies became desperate, with pleas of 'just send the money'. Eventually he called round to her house late at night, in deep snow, and was surprised to find her safely at home.[38]

Clearly, most people will know if their loved one is

travelling, which will give them an inkling of whether the email is genuine. And many scams have been adapted from previous ones – copy and paste the SOS text into Google and other versions will probably come up. But it costs virtually nothing to send out millions of emails, so even if just one person falls for the ruse, it can be worthwhile for the scammer.

Another notorious trick is the Nigerian 419 scam – the number refers to the section of Nigerian law that it violates. Bulk emails are sent out from hacked accounts saying that the sender needs help transferring a large amount of money out of Nigeria or another country. The victim is asked to cover the cost of transferring the money and told that later they will receive a larger sum back. If the victim pays, they are told more money is required because of complications.[39] As with other email scams, it's so cheap to do that netting just one victim makes the criminal venture profitable.[40]

MALWARE

Short for 'malicious software', malware is any software that installs itself without your permission. It hides on your machine and you often don't spot the intrusion.

VIRUSES

Computer viruses are generally spread through downloads on the Internet, email attachments or instant messages. A virus can enter your email program and then send out emails to all your contacts to spread itself. It can also corrupt or delete data – at the worst, it can erase your entire hard drive.[41] Disseminating a computer virus is a crime. Some hackers create viruses just to cause problems and see what happens but others work with cybercriminals. They may use the virus to access your personal information or steal disk space.[42]

WORMS
A worm is similar to a virus and causes damage in the same way, but it can spread without human assistance. It breaks in through a vulnerability in the system.[43]

TROJANS
Cybercriminals may get into people's computers using a Trojan horse – a program inside a seemingly normal photo or document attached to an email. The Trojan gives the fraudster secret control, turning your machine into a zombie computer that they can command. They can use your address book to send out spam emails to all their contacts or turn your machine into a weapon for a Distributed Denial of Service (DDoS) attack against a website (see page 82).

SPYWARE
This is software that changes your computer without your permission. It includes adware, which auto-matically displays advertisements and may track the websites you visit to work out which ads to send. It can change the web browser's home page and may make it hard to restore your computer to the original settings. Spyware may also use a keylogger to record your keystrokes to acquire personal information and details of how you use your computer.[44]

SCAREWARE
If you've ever seen an alarming pop-up purporting to warn you about viruses or spyware detected on

your computer, then you've spotted scareware. It's designed to frighten the user into clicking on a link that downloads bogus software. It may lead you to purchase fake security products, thereby releasing your credit card details to the fraudster, who could use it to gain access to your account.[45]

Phishing

Although it's annoying, spam is legal if the vendor is selling a legal product, but phishing is attempted fraud and it's illegal. A spear phishing email pretends to be from an individual whom you know, or a legitimate business such as a bank, and includes a request to click on a link and confirm your username and password, or your card details, perhaps to confirm a transaction. When you do this, the fraudster receives your security details.

THE PHISHER'S GUIDE

1. Buy bulk freshly hacked emails.

2. Buy Dark Mailer – super-fast bulk email software.

3. Buy proxy servers for anonymity – they allow you to make indirect connections to other network servers through an intermediary.

4. Design a new bank webpage to mirror a real one.

5. Put in a pop-up box that doesn't go away until a card and pin number are entered.

6. Set up an email address for victims' replies.

7. Watch the card and pin numbers roll in.[46]

Banks generally won't cover the lost funds if you inadvertently give out your details to a scammer in a phishing attack. In the Philippines, consultant Carlos D. Malibiran lost P 159,000 (£2,322) between July and October 2014. Without his knowledge, the monthly consultancy fees paid into his bank account were being withdrawn by online transfer.[47] Malibiran complained to the bank but was told that because his account credentials had been compromised, there was nothing they could do. He was disappointed that banks promote online banking but seem unable to protect their customers' deposits from phishing attacks.

STEALING IDENTITIES

Our identity online is just a bundle of numbers and other identifiers in databases owned by governments and companies. If a fraudster gets hold of these numbers they can pose as the victim to their great financial advantage. In the United States, people do not have ID cards but their Social Security number acts as a unique identifier. Taxes are collected on the basis of this ID, and the government and private institutions use it to keep track of people. If you have somebody's Social Security number, you can get access to all their documents and steal their identity.

One 18-year-old student was alarmed to receive a Notice of Adjustment letter in 2014 informing her that she owed $20,000 (£13,966) in taxes for the past three years. She was still dependent on her parents and only had a part-time job in a bakery. How could she possibly owe so much money? She contacted the Internal Revenue Service (IRS) and requested a copy of her tax return. When she received it, she noticed that her name and Social Security number were correct but the taxes were not. She couldn't believe a low-income student could be a target of identity theft. How did it happen?

Often, people leave the unwelcome task of filing their tax return to the last minute. The US tax office has revealed cases where identity fraudsters have filed other people's taxes first to benefit from the fraudulent tax refunds. In the case above, the fraudster had filed the student's tax return before her, and had listed taxable deductions for educational materials, including a computer. This freaked her out – did the fraudster know this much about her or had they made an educated guess based on her age? It was worrying to know that the scammer had her name and social security number and could use them for other illegal purposes. She checked whether anyone had tried to take out loans based on her identity. The scammer could easily have taken out a credit card and run up huge bills or sold her information on the Darknet for other criminals to use. Fortunately, there was no evidence of further cybercrime.

Hoping to lay the matter to rest, she filled out a form for the IRS stating that she had been a victim of identity theft. After an anxious six months, the IRS informed her that the matter had been sorted out. But she never discovered how the security of her data had been breached.[48] Cases like these are now encouraging people to file their tax returns early!

THE IDENTITY THIEF

With a stolen credit card, a criminal can contact the issuing bank and say 'I've moved house – this is my new address.' With the card and new address, he gets a new driving licence with his picture but the victim's name. Using the driving licence, he gets a Social Security number, again with the victim's name and his photo. Now he can open a bank account and take out loans using the victim's credit record. As the debts roll in, the bank contacts the original credit card holder, who suddenly realizes his ID has been stolen.[49]

It's harder to steal identity in Europe than in the UK or United States because Europeans have an ID card with a unique number. Usually only governments have access to it while private companies, including banks, do not. European companies have stricter rules regarding the information that businesses can keep about their customers, and in 2017 the rules were due to become stricter. Under new regulations, in order to share data with a third party, the data controller will have to inform individuals that their data is being shared – and they will have the right to object to this.[50]

Biometrics – unique identifiers?

Automated biometric systems were introduced in the early 2000s and hailed as a fail-safe identification method because everyone's fingerprints and irises are unique. Countries such as the United States, Australia and the United Kingdom collect biometric information for travellers' passports. Such information is also used on mobile devices for identification. But hackers have devised methods of accessing mobiles, stealing stored fingerprints[51] and reconstructing them from digital templates. Researcher Javier Galbally at the Universidad Autónoma, in Madrid, Spain, has shown that a scanned iris can be hacked, too:

'New research shows that building an eyeball from a digital iris template is ... plausible ... Iris scanners take an image of

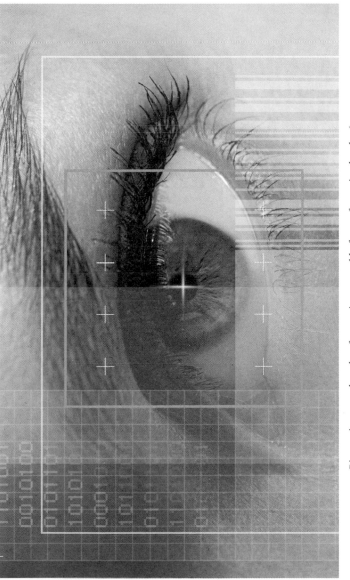

Biometrics were thought of as an impenetrable form of security, but hackers have found ways to fool fingerprint scanners and even iris scanners.

the eye, stretch the iris out into a rectangle, and then create a template of 0s and 1s called an "iriscode" ... By making an image out of the stored iriscode, stretching it into a circle, and feeding it back into the system, Galbally's team was able to get into the system with an 87 percent success rate.[52]

If your credit card is stolen, you can get a new credit card, but you can't get a new fingerprint or iris. It's like using one password forever, which cannot be changed.[53] Researchers have worked to develop counter-measures that enable biometric systems to detect fake samples, using 'liveness detection' to identify the differences between real and fake traits.[54] Nevertheless, it appears that biometric systems are not the panacea for secure identification they were once hoped to be.

BREACHING THE BANKS

If you're a fraudster after money, why not cut out the customers and head straight to the top – the banks themselves? The financial industry is better at security than most industries but there have been some spectacular breaches.

Turkish cybercrime mastermind Ercan Findikoglu was allegedly responsible for one of them. Extradited to the United States in 2015, he was accused of having organized cyberattacks worth US $55 million (£39 million). Prosecutors alleged that he hacked into three large credit- and debit-card payment processors, two of which were owned by MasterCard. Once into their networks, he hugely increased the balances of Visa and MasterCard pre-paid debit cards. Then he sent out the stolen debit-card details to 'cashing crews' around the world, who took the money out of ATMs in thousands of withdrawals. In the biggest attack, during two days in February 2013, hackers

Bank Muscat in Oman was the subject of one of the worst cyberattacks on the financial sector in February 2013, resulting in the loss of US $40 million.

gained access to cards issued by Bank Muscat in Oman; cash crews in 24 countries carried out 36,000 withdrawals, totalling an incredible US $40 million (£28 million). Findiloglu and other senior organizers were alleged to have received huge chunks of the proceeds. In March 2016 Findikoglu pleaded guilty to charges related to the cyberattack spree.[55]

The Carbanak attack

In February 2015, Russian computer-security company Kaspersky Lab[56] revealed that hackers had infiltrated a bank in Ukraine and stolen a whopping US $1 billion (£700 million) over two years from financial institutions worldwide. The highly organized and well-coordinated Carbanak attack[57] was carried out by a multinational gang of cybercriminals from Russia, Ukraine, other parts of Europe and China. The cybergang used spear phishing to encourage an employee to click on a link in a spam email, which infected the computer with Carbanak malware and allowed the hackers into the bank's internal network. There they found the administrators' computers for video surveillance so they could record the screens of the staff who were transferring cash. Then they were able to transfer money from users' accounts to their own. Each robbery took two to four months, from infecting the first computer in the bank's network to cashing out the money, and each raid netted the fraudsters up to US $10 million (£7 million).

Sometimes, the gang inflated account balances before taking the extra funds. For example, if an account contained £100, they changed it to £1,000 and grabbed the extra £900. The account holder wouldn't have realized their account had been compromised because their balance remained £100.

The attackers also took control of ATMs and programmed them to dispense cash at a particular time, when one of the fraudsters would be standing by as the ATM disgorged cash like an enthusiastic fruit machine.[58]

Carding

Carding began in the early 2000s with the development of the skimmer – a big breakthrough for fraudsters worldwide. A skimming device is fixed to an ATM, where it reads and stores the magnetic strips on customers' debit or credit cards so they can be transferred to blank cards and used to withdraw cash from the victims' accounts. A hidden camera records customer PINs. Credit-card cloning involved minimal resources and risk, and it developed rapidly in the chaotic environment of post-Soviet eastern Europe in the early 2000s, where many were unemployed with poor job prospects. In 2002, enterprising criminal Dmitriy Golubov (known as Script) from Odessa set up CarderPlanet, a website for trading stolen bank data. With high levels of credit-card ownership in the United States, UK, Japan and Canada, young eastern Europeans realized there was lots of money sloshing around that they could steal.[59] The Russian police didn't seem to care as long as the carders didn't operate in Russia. As Belorussian carder 'Police Dog' noted: 'If we didn't make a mess on our own doorstop [sic] then our local cops and intelligence services didn't have a problem with us.'[60]

ESCROW: ENSURING THIEVES PAY UP

Known as Boa, Ukrainian crook Roman Vega developed the website Boa Factory, which produced counterfeit passports and ID cards, and cloned credit cards. Given that everyone using the site was a thief, it was essential to devise a secure system to ensure people got paid. He came up with the inventive escrow system. The vendor provided the escrow officer with samples of the wares – some 'dumps' and 'wholes' (credit-card numbers and PIN numbers). The officer tested them out and if they provided cash, he released money to the vendor and the dumps and wholes to the buyer.[61] This cunning system was later adopted by drugs traders on the Darknet (see page 129).

Both Boa and Script were captured after several years, but carding spread across the globe and became increasingly sophisticated.[62] In 2014, the European ATM Security Team issued a report, based on data from 19 countries,[63] alerting the police and public to the existence of new, barely visible, slimline skimmers. Some remained in place for five days before discovery, stealing hundreds of customers' details. A tiny dot over the keypad is a pinhole, with a camera lens behind it. Criminals have inserted the camera to photograph customers' PIN numbers as they key them in, and covered it with a blank grey tile. Another component fitted over the card slot records the magnetic strip. ATM users were warned to be ever more vigilant when accessing their cash.

BAD BUSINESS

Online commerce is burgeoning worldwide; in China, it grew by 40 per cent in 2015. Business crime in cyberspace has followed the upward trend, creating a vast marketplace for the sale of counterfeit goods. Cybercriminals also target business operations through wire fraud, the false inflation of share prices and the creation of phantom employees.

Fake websites and counterfeit goods

Some fake websites are relatively harmless, created for amusement. Check out Dog Island at www.thedogisland.com, where dogs live free from humans. The one expensive item for sale – the Leather Empathy Training Leash at $6,099 (£4,260) – is fortunately out of stock.[64] Bonsai Kitten at http://ding.net/bonsaikitten/index.html purports to explain the art of modifying the shape of your pet, while Save the Tree Octopus at http://zapatopi.net/treeoctopus/ sells posters, mugs and T-shirts emblazoned with images of this mythical creature.

Other false websites imitate those of major companies; they pretend to offer goods and services but simply take your money and send nothing. Fake online auctions are particularly common in the United States, accounting for about half of all online fraud cases.[65] These are transactional crimes – the victims willingly give up their payment details. So there's not much they can do about it once they find out they've been conned.

China is notorious for pirated products and has been heavily criticized for the large number of counterfeit goods sold online. A report to Chinese lawmakers in November 2015 indicated that more than 40 per cent of goods sold online were imitations or shoddy.[66] The US government put the giant e-commerce company Alibaba Group, which sells branded goods to the Chinese, on its e-commerce blacklist in December 2016, stating that Alibaba was selling large quantities of counterfeit products through its marketplace Taobao.[67]

Japan and South Korea also experience high levels of this kind of fraud. In 2015, Takahashi from Chiba, Japan, was arrested for selling clothing with fake autographs of members of the Osaka girl band NMB48. Among others, two 59-year-old men had successfully bid for NMB48 bathing suits, paying 210,000 yen (US$1,775/£1,212) in total. (Without excusing the crime, one wonders why a man would pay £600 for a swimsuit with a name on it.) Takahashi claimed members of the band had worn the bathing suits and other items and autographed them but police alleged he had forged them himself. The suspect soon confessed to the crime. Police believed he had made about 2.5 million yen (US$21,125/£14,425) in a year from auctioning around 180 items.[68]

Defrauding businesses

When cybercriminals target business operations, their profits can be vast and the damage to the company's coffers and reputation significant. Wire fraud, pump-and-dump and payroll fraud are some of the common tactics. Wire fraud is a sophisticated operation in which fraudsters send emails pretending to be senior executives of the finance departments of companies, requesting that employees wire money overseas to a fraudulent bank account. Most commercial insurance companies don't cover the loss because the employee wired the money voluntarily.[69] Hackers with stockmarket nous will go on to financial sites, buy up shares in low-value stocks and spread information to artificially inflate share prices. They may give out false insider knowledge that a particular stock is about to spike. The stock rockets in value, the cybercriminals sell their holdings for a big profit, and the share price subsequently collapses.[70] Another tactic is to infiltrate companies' automated payroll systems to add phantom employees and pay them each month. Their salary goes to 'money mules', who for a small fee will pass on the cash to a bank far away.

Inside job

Payroll fraud is often an inside job, committed by an employee in the Human Resources (HR) department who creates phantom employees with time sheets in cyberspace and pays their salary into his or her account.

The parents of Matthew 'Sonny Boy' Chester owned Chester Electronics Inc. (CEI), and the Chester family owned all the company's stock. CEI employed office staff and many low-paid immigrants on the factory floor. Sonny Boy owned a share and was in charge of HR and payroll. He had a well-paying job but wanted more. Over nine years he created 344 'zombie' employees by issuing pay cheques to employees who were absent or had left. It was easy to get away with falsifying the computer records because no one else looked at them. The company paid salaries with cheques, which were generated by an outside payroll vendor and sent to Sonny Boy. He extracted the fraudulent ones, endorsed them to himself by writing on the back and paid them into his own account. In this way, he netted himself more than half a million dollars (£350,000).

The false records caused huge difficulties for the real people behind the zombie employees. When the records were passed to the income tax authority, it appeared that the employees had a higher income than they really did. One man found it hard to apply for public housing assistance because his stated income was too high – but of course he'd never received the inflated sum.

One day, Sonny Boy's sister Maisie, who managed the corporation's finances, checked the payroll records. She looked at the front and back of the cheques and spotted the cheques endorsed over to Sonny Boy. After running a 10-year spot check and finding many more, she employed an outside accounting firm to run an audit.

Maisie presented her findings to the family, and Sonny Boy apologized profusely. The family didn't want to go to the police but Maisie did, which pitted her against the entire family. Following a court case, Sonny Boy had to pay back the money and spent 23 months in jail.[71]

FIGHTING FRAUD

Governments and companies employ security experts to improve their defences against cyberattack with technological wizardry. A vast global cybersecurity industry has developed, led by companies such as Kaspersky Lab, FireEye and Palo Alto Networks.[72] Alongside these efforts, governments have introduced mass surveillance and laws against cybercrime to try to resist the rising tide of criminal activity.

Technical solutions

Banks love e-banking because it's cheap for them – it has allowed them to close down many branches and reduce staff. They need to be seen to be tackling bank fraud so that customers trust online banking. Increasingly, banks expect users to remember long passwords and security codes. They're trying to encourage people to use mobile banking but it can be hard to enter complicated passwords correctly on a small screen while on the go.

Some banks have been exploring alternative forms of verification. German banks have developed the photoTAN app, which uses an app downloaded to a phone or computer so that only customers can view the emailed account information. Their transaction information is turned into an image, which looks like a jumble of coloured squares. The customer takes a photo of the image and the app decodes it. Google is working to improve CAPTCHA, designed to check that a real person has filled in a form. It developed reCAPTCHA: a user simply needs to click in a box saying 'I am not a robot'. However, in April 2016 a team of security experts revealed that they had discovered vulnerabilities in the Google and Facebook reCAPTCHA systems. Verification techniques have to be updated continually to be effective.[73]

Captcha stands for 'Completely Automated Public Turing test to tell Computers and Humans Apart'. Text distortion is commonly used to make sure that the user is a real human being, and not a computer program.

Improving privacy online can help to reduce phishing emails. But it's quite hard to use encryption programs such as Pretty Good Privacy (PGP). Google and Dropbox have backed the development of Simply Secure, an open-source (freely available) program to make it simpler for users to protect themselves.[74] Run by Sara 'Scout' Sinclair Brody, the project's tagline is 'Security's got to be easy and intuitive, or it won't work.'[75] Simply Secure is open-source so other people can scrutinize it and work collaboratively to improve it. The aim is to provide easy-to-use privacy-preserving software rather than expecting users to adopt specialist tools.[76]

Mass surveillance

Many countries, including the United States, UK and Germany, are adopting mass surveillance – collecting online data records of the entire population. Governments argue that since cybercrime is growing exponentially, such measures are vital in the fight against it. But the use of surveillance is contested. As a Human Rights Watch report in 2014 noted, 'The US and UK governments contend that to find a needle in a haystack security agencies must collect the haystack.'[77] Also, criminals could develop bulk surveillance for their own purposes or hack government-sponsored surveillance. Widespread monitoring of the surface net could drive more criminal communications to the Darknet (see Chapter 6). So it is not clear that mass surveillance can stop cybercrime.

Laying down the law

Individual countries have introduced laws to try to keep up with novel cybercrimes. Japan is often ahead of the United States or Europe in cracking down on these illicit activities. In 2014, Japanese police officers arrested 381 people and seized 118,464 items. But they face limitations. The counterfeiters frequently run their operations offshore, so Japanese authorities have no jurisdiction over them. The European Business Council Intellectual Property Rights Committee in Japan recommends trying to stop such goods being sold in the country and checking online auction sites to see if the goods are genuine – yet this is extremely time-consuming and costly. The counterfeit sites are often set up in China where enforcement is weaker; the police can tell the sites originate in China because the Japanese text is not perfect and the prices are very low. However, tensions between China and Japan make it to tricky to cooperate over fighting cybercrime.

The Japanese police are also hampered by the rights of banks and credit-card companies not to divulge their clients' details. Most payments are made by direct transfer to bank accounts or by credit card. The Japanese police cannot get the seller's account closed because they don't know the account number. If they know the number of a fraudulent account, they can ask the bank to close it down, but the bank does not have to comply. Such accounts are often opened by Chinese students in Japan, who sell them to fraudsters in China. To stop credit-card transactions, the police can try to contact the card company and ask it to reject payments to the seller but the company does not have to agree.

The United Arab Emirates (UAE) has also tried to crack down on cybercrime. In 2012, a new Cyber Law aimed to protect individuals and companies from cybercrime, creating severe penalties for crimes such as fraud and forgery. In one case in 2014, fraudsters set up a website with the name of a company based in Abu Dhabi. The fake website had the same name as the genuine website but ended with .org instead of .com. It was a startlingly professional fake site, with the names of all the board members and the CEO of the company and details of the company's areas of expertise. The fraudsters contacted individuals and companies to offer investment services, using a fraudulent email address with the name of a senior member of the company. One victim was taken in and transferred money to the fake company. The Cyber Law was used to close the fraudulent website immediately.[78]

The same law has been used to police morality in the UAE. In 2015, two footballers and a website owner stood trial in Abu Dhabi accused of using telecommunications to breach public morals. A film of an angry footballer hurling offensive insults and making 'obscene moves' went viral on social media. One suspect confessed to shouting abuse, the second to filming it; the third claimed that he had published part of the clip but that his website had been hacked in order to publish the second part.[79] The footballers were given three-month suspended sentences.[80]

This incident indicates how hard it is to fight cybercrime across national boundaries because different countries perceive crime differently. Morality issues such as those in the above UAE case might not be counted as cybercrime in other countries, where there is more tolerance towards the bad behaviour of highly popular sports personalities. Some international laws have been passed, such as the Council of Europe Cybercrime Convention, ratified by 51 states by December 2016. But international cybercrime treaties need to be ratified by all countries to be effective.[81]

THE CYBERCRIME CHALLENGE

According to a 2015 report by Experian about companies based in Europe, the Middle East and Africa (EMEA), 'Seventy-eight percent identified online fraud as the most challenging fraud problem they are facing right now.'[82]

People may have become more aware of email and phishing scams and the dangers of malware, but it only takes one user in a network to click on a rogue link for the entire network to be compromised. As nations increasingly turn to e-government, uploading the population's employment and health records, the threat of identity theft grows. Despite impressive technology to use unique biometric data as identification, hackers have discovered how to crack it. Banks have highly developed security systems but determined hackers can find vulnerabilities and all systems are prone to user error. The banks' own internal security systems can be turned against them, as indicated by the sophisticated Carbanak attack in which the bank's own video surveillance was used by the fraudsters to record staff transactions. As Sergey Golovanov, principal security researcher at Kaspersky Lab's global research and analysis team noted, 'These attacks … underline the fact that criminals will exploit any vulnerability in any system. It also highlights the fact that no sector can consider itself immune to attack and [they] must constantly address their security procedures.'[83] Naturally, he wants to promote Kaspersky's services, but his point stands nevertheless.

E-commerce has encouraged the proliferation of counterfeit goods – the most sophisticated fake sites can be difficult to differentiate from the genuine ones. The Internet has become a playground for inventive fraudsters who find novel markets for products such as fake autographed swimwear. But using debit and credit cards in ATMs without exercising vigilance can be just as risky as using them on the Internet. The carding fraternity has been remarkably innovative in its ventures, producing discreet skimmers and an escrow system for secure online payments.

The electronic management of company systems has

facilitated payroll scams; when nobody is checking through individual physical records and an external company pays the wages, it is relatively easy to create ghost employees, especially for insiders.

What can be done? Anti-fraud software clearly has a role to play but will never be more than one step ahead of the fraudsters. Improving online privacy is a promising way forward (see page 158), but would need to be widely adopted to prove effective. Using mass surveillance may prove to be like using a sledgehammer to crack a nut. Gathering data is straightforward but analysing it to pinpoint criminal activity accurately could absorb vast resources. Trying to stop the sale of counterfeit goods also requires phenomenal effort, and even if fraudulent sites are closed down, they can quickly be set up again. It really is a never-ending cycle.[84]

If ratified by significant numbers of countries, international cybercrime laws would make it easier to track down fraudsters operating from servers around the globe and could allow police forces to catch greater numbers of them. Yet as more of our transactions are carried out online, the opportunities for cybercrime grow, and the potential rewards increase. The lure of lucrative gains will always prove attractive to people prepared to act outside the law. Whatever brilliant security innovations are developed to prevent crime, enterprising fraudsters are likely to find a way to bypass them.

CHAPTER 3

COPYRIGHT OR
THE RIGHT TO COPY?

Aaron Swartz was the co-founder of Reddit, one of the biggest global social-networking news sites. In 2011, the 25-year-old was arrested and charged for taking his laptop to the Massachusetts Institute of Technology (MIT) and downloading lots of academic journal articles from the digital library JSTOR – articles that were freely available from MIT. Swartz broke the law but he didn't hack JSTOR or release the articles on the Internet, and JSTOR did not opt to pursue charges. Yet the young man was faced with a totally disproportionate 35-year jail sentence and US $1 million (£686,700) in fines. In 2013, unable to cope with the extreme pressure of the charges, Aaron Swartz tragically took his own life.[85]

Is file sharing a crime? According to the media industry, sharing media files is digital piracy. The livelihoods of millions around the world depend on creating music, writing books and shooting movies, and thousands of companies are based on marketing them to the public. It is illegal to share this material for free, and copyright laws are essential to

Aaron Swartz in 2007. The suicide of this extremely gifted young man was a tragedy. In 2015, a documentary was made about his life, entitled The Internet's Own Boy.

protect intellectual property. On the other side, information freedom activists see file sharing as a vital tool for spreading knowledge for the benefit of society. It's their mission to break through security settings and share music, films and books freely, in an attempt to bring back the idealistic days of the early Internet when ideas flourished without the intrusion of the market. In their view, 'information wants to be free'.

COPYRIGHT LAWS

The United States has been at the forefront at developing legislation to protect intellectual property. The Digital Millennium Copyright Act (DMCA) of 1998 made it illegal to circumvent the Digital Rights Management technology that controls the access to copyrighted material. The DMCA Act also has take-down provisions that limit freedom of information – people can demand that a site takes down material that they object to. In 2008, the Church of Scientology used this law to demand the removal of 4,000 YouTube videos that it deemed to be critical of the religious sect, and YouTube complied with the request.[86] Other organizations have taken up the copyright protection challenge; the Recording Industry Association of America (RIAA) has been zealous in pursuing online music pirates.[87]

But some attempts to bring in harsher copyright laws have failed. Signed by eight countries in 2011[88] but not ratified by sufficient countries for it to come into effect, the Anti Counterfeiting Trade Agreement (ACTA) was a tougher version of the Digital Millennium Copyright Act. It aimed to make copyright infringement a criminal offence and encouraged Internet Service Providers (ISPs) to track users. ACTA was criticized for its potential impact on freedom of expression and privacy. The US Stop Online Piracy Act (SOPA) was stopped by a huge popular campaign in 2012. This proposed law called for search engines such as Google to prevent sites that allowed peer-to-peer (P2P) sharing (see below) from appearing when users typed their name into the search box.[89] As part of a mass protest including petitions and tweet campaigns, around 75,000 webpages were changed to black, with links asking people to protest about SOPA to their representatives.

INFORMATION FREEDOM

Opposing copyright laws are information freedom activists like Jérémie Zimmermann, the French co-founder of Internet freedom advocacy group La Quadrature du Net. He argues that file sharing is good for society and should not be criminalized. People can share files through a P2P network[90] – a decentralized communication model. Rather than a client making a service request and the server meeting the request, each computer is both a client and a server that can provide anonymous routing of Internet traffic. It means that computer users can share materials directly with others without them passing through a central server. P2P networks are typically used for media sharing so they are associated with software piracy and the violation of copyright laws. They first became popular in the late 1990s. In 1999, music-sharing site Napster hit the Internet. According to Zimmermann, music lovers shared the songs they enjoyed and went to gigs to hear the bands. They publicized their favourite artists and spread the word so the bands' fan base grew.[91] It was not a form of stealing. Napster was shut down in 2001 but other sites have taken its place. In the early 2000s, the BitTorrent communications protocol appeared and became popular for illegally downloading music and movies. Sites such as The Pirate Bay, founded in 2003, became the go-to site for downloading pirated movies using BitTorrent.

*BitTorrent became the essential piece of software
for downloading pirate copies of music and movies.*

BITTORRENT – ONLINE PIRACY OR INTERNET FREEDOM?

In 2001 US computer programmer Bram Cohen worked out how to transfer files extremely rapidly from one computer to another. Many computers around the world transferred bits of the same file simultaneously. He made the software open-source so anyone could download it. In 2004 Cohen launched his company BitTorrent to make legal use of the technology. As the CEO Eric Klinker has commented, the aim was to 'hard-code certain human rights into the Internet, whether that's the right to privacy or a right to free speech'. So how does BitTorrent make its money? A main source is user clicks. The company offers free BitTorrent software. When you download it, you're asked if you'd like to install a toolbar that switches your default browser and home pages to Yahoo or Ask. com, and BitTorrent gets paid every time a user switches.[92]

CAMPAIGNS AGAINST COPYRIGHT

Another prong in the online freedom campaign is attacking the copyright enforcers. In 2010, freedom of information hacktivist group Anonymous had reason to believe that the pro-copyright Motion Picture Association of America (MPAA) had hired an Indian software company called Aiplex to attack The Pirate Bay. Aiplex had used Distributed Denial of Service (DDoS) attacks (see page 82) against the site; the Anons felt it was justified to retaliate against a company that was itself using illegal tactics and was even boasting about it.[93] Despite a lack of hard evidence that Aiplex was employed by MPAA,[94] Anonymous launched Operation Payback, using DDoS attacks and SQL injection (see pages 71–72) to get root access to Aiplex's server and defacing its website with the message, 'Payback is a Bitch'.

The MPAA itself, with strong anti-DDoS protection, was too big a target for Anonymous, which now turned its sights on ACS:Law, a British company that sent thousands of threatening letters to alleged file sharers, demanding payment for illegal downloads.[95] Anons were able to take down this site in just two minutes. However, Andrew Crossley, the head of the law firm, made light of the attack.

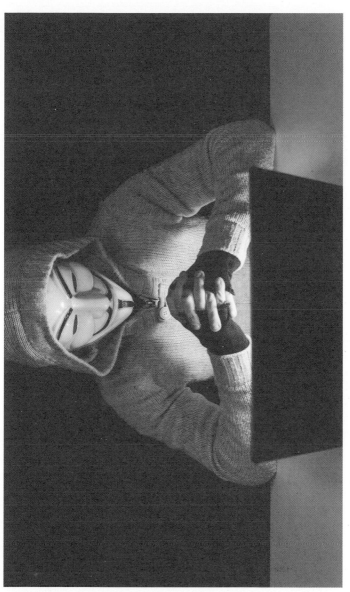

A typical image of an Anonymous activist wearing a Guy Fawkes mask to preserve anonymity. The mask has become a well-known symbol of the hacktivist group.

In a conversation with technology website The Register, he scoffed, 'It was only down for a few hours. I have far more concern over the fact of my train turning up 10 minutes late or having to queue for a coffee than them wasting my time with this sort of rubbish.'[96]

This clear provocation to Anonymous was all that was needed for activists to redouble their attacks. When ACS:Law's web team tried to restore the site, they accidentally posted all their records, including emails and passwords, in directories on their website's front page. Anons happily released all the data on The Pirate Bay. The extent of ACS:Law's bullying was revealed; for example, the company was writing to married men to ask them to pay around £500 for downloading gay porn.[97] Crossley's bravado had been mistaken. The revelations destroyed trust in the company to protect its data and within months it had closed down.

A MIDDLE GROUND?

Could there be a managed process to allow more digital freedom? In Europe, the Digital Single Market Strategy, due to be delivered by the end of 2016, aims to reduce national differences in copyright law and allow greater online access to cultural works across the European Union (EU). As President of the European Commission Jean-Claude Juncker promised, 'I believe that we must make much better use of the great opportunities offered by digital technologies, which know no borders. To do so, we will need to have the courage to break down national silos in telecoms regulation, in copyright and data protection legislation, in the management of radio waves and in the application of competition law.'[98]

People can travel freely across the EU to live and work, so it seems logical that they should be able to access information from all European nations online. Rapidly changing technology allows users to seek out the content they desire regardless of whether it is available legally. Perhaps this could be a case of the law racing to catch up and legalize what people are doing anyway.

The argument over copyright or the right to copy is essentially an argument about the role of the Internet – is it a tool for free expression or an arm of global commerce, where information is property just like material goods? Can fair copyright rules be devised? Attempts to introduce laws such as SOPA have failed because their opponents have seen them as draconian breaches of privacy. And attempts to impose the rules are hampered because they are not universally respected internationally. There have been moves to extend international copyright laws, such as ACTA, but if countries do not ratify them, they cannot become effective. Extending digital rights from national to continental level, as proposed in the EU, could be a way forward. Whatever the law says, file sharing is as popular as ever. What does this mean for the producers of music, books and movies? They will surely continue to publicize and sell their output online, hoping that increased shares of their wares, whether legal or not, will increase their exposure and popularity in the real world. And as we'll see in Chapter 7, it is likely that more will move their operations to the Darknet, away from the control of the regulators.

CHAPTER 4

CYBERCRIME: SUBVERSION

In 2015, the Canadian government introduced Bill C-51, granting extensive new powers to law enforcement and intelligence organizations. It allowed them to share among government departments the personal information of anyone suspected of being a threat to national security – but the definition of a 'threat' was extremely vague.[99] Self-appointed privacy guardians Anonymous mounted a publicity campaign against the bill, but it failed to gain traction in the media. So the Anons resorted to their traditional tactic of Distributed Denial of Service (DDoS) attacks. D-Day for OpCyberPrivacy was 17 June and they reported:[100]

'Anonymous attacked Canadian government servers after Anonymous uploaded a couple of videos against the approval of anti-terror law C-51, which hurts both Internet privacy and Anonymous. As per this law, Canadian security intelligence will gain immense power, and will be able to violate any individual's Internet privacy whenever they want to. Anonymous took down the following websites of [the] Canadian government:

- *Online portal Canada.ca*
- *Department of finance*
- *Treasury board*
- *And other websites of major departments.* [101]

Anonymous claimed, 'Canada's cybersecurity agency was equipped with infantile online protection and it was shocking how quickly we were able to disable them [sic] entirely.'[102] Not only was Anonymous protesting against increased surveillance but it was also flagging up the Canadian government's failure to protect the population's vital income and health data.

This kind of attack is increasingly common. From 2000, a plethora of subversive movements arose: anti-globalization and animal rights campaigns; hacktivist actions; social media protest movements in Russia, China and Iran; and the Arab Spring. All aimed to undermine the authority of their government and they all organized in cyberspace.[103] Much subversion is legal but DDoS and other cyberattacks are crimes under the law.

A discussion of legality versus legitimacy is crucial here. During the Arab Spring, protesters questioned the legitimacy of dictatorial regimes and believed it was right to expose them regardless of whether the campaigners' tactics were legal. On the other hand, in a liberal democracy, it is healthy to have a certain level of subversion – it demonstrates that the system is robust and there is freedom of expression. In time, ideas considered subversive can become mainstream; a few decades ago, it was subversive to support gay rights. Subversive activity usually has limited goals. It does not aim to overthrow a government but merely to point out the failings of an organization or a particular important individual.[104] If governments clamp down too heavily on challenging perspectives, they may shift towards authoritarianism; their actions may be legal but their legitimacy could be called into question.

Subversion has always existed but online groups differ from traditional face-to-face organizations. Online groups have far higher membership mobility – it is easy to join them and just as easy to drop out. Leaders have less of a role because it is hard to control and discipline an amorphous organization in cyberspace.[105] And while it is simple to start a movement with a call to action on a forum, it is hard to succeed. These factors help to explain the huge explosion of movements and wide variety of subversive ideas on the Internet.

Online subversion includes individual actions such as jailbreaking to free products from the restrictions imposed by their manufacturer and group efforts to hack major organizations to expose security failures, corruption and human rights abuses. A major subversive movement, Anonymous first emerged as a bunch of hackers who were in it for the lulz (see page 21) but moved towards political activism. During the Arab Spring of 2011, an upsurge in online subversion, supported by Anonymous, paved the way for uprisings in the real world. Governments have adopted strong-arm tactics to counter online subversion, adopting similar illegal tactics to their enemies and imposing heavy penalties on offenders in a never-ending battle for the control of cyberspace.

JAILBREAKING

Professor Gabriella Coleman is an expert on hacking culture and its socio-political implications, focusing particularly on the free software movement and the digital protest group Anonymous. In her 2015 book *Hacker, Hoaxer, Whistleblower, Spy: The Many Faces of Anonymous*, one of the issues she explores is the geohot case. In 2011 geohot (George Hotz) posted jailbreaking instructions for the PS3 on his website. On his altered device, he could do backups, play games faster directly from his hard drive, watch videos and load the open-source GNU/Linux operating system (OS). He could also play pirated games. The new set-up allowed him to innovate and learn on his PS3. When the UK British Broadcasting Company (BBC) interviewed geohot about his exploits, he rephrased the popular hackers' motto: '[PS3] is supposed to be *unhackable*, but *nothing is unhackable*.'[106]

'Jailbreaking' is the subversion of a product – modifying a device so it can be used in a different way. Jailbreakers believe it is their right to use their property as they wish. They post the instructions so others can enjoy the same freedom; they're not profiting from their work but simply sharing the information. Sony didn't see geohot's actions in quite the same way. It sued him for violating the Computer Fraud and Abuse Act in a lawsuit that also targeted other hackers and 100 people who had viewed geohot's jailbreaking instructions. YouTube was requested to release information on all those who had done so.[107]

Science-fiction writer Cory Doctorow thought it was: 'absurd and unjust for a gargantuan multinational to use its vast legal resources to crush a lone hacker whose "crime" is to figure out how to do (legal) stuff with his own property.'[108] Yet Sony alleged that distributing the PS3 root keys and jailbreak tools allowed users to play illegal copies of PS3 video games and that the keys were worth 'far more than

$5,000 [£3,470] over any 1-year period', potentially reducing the profitability of the product for Sony.[109]

So should you be able to do what you like with your property or not? There are arguments for 'jailing' a product to prevent alternative uses. Apple's iPhone can only run Apple software from the App Store. This allows the company to recoup the cost of its investment by requiring you to buy its apps. Restricting you to the Apple OS can improve security because you can only download software from trusted sources. It also makes it harder for you to make unlawful use of legally downloaded materials.

On the other hand, you bought the device and perhaps you prefer a different OS – why should the company decide which software you use? If you jailbreak your device, it is your own, unpaid work so why should it matter to the company? You might even patch vulnerabilities yourself. It is true that using the freed PS3 console made it possible to play pirated games. But any computer can be used to access illegal materials.

Sony was targeted because it used to let people run Linux on its PlayStations but then reversed the decision and locked down the device so it was extremely difficult to switch. But the PS3 was hacked anyway, and even though Sony sued the perpetrators, the jailbreaking information is still available. As of 2016, Linux could be installed on the PS4.[110] However secret companies try to keep their technical details, hackers are sure to find a way in and subvert products for their own purposes.

UNDERMINING TRUST

Hacking major companies is a surefire way to undermine trust in them. Highly skilled intelligent individuals may hack simply to show off their technical prowess. Whether or not they steal data, it is a criminal offence.

Cyberattack: TalkTalk

The year of 2015 was a bad one for British telecoms giant TalkTalk. In February, the company confirmed hackers had stolen some of its 4 million customers' personal data. This was nothing compared to the huge cyberattack on the morning of 23 October. Hackers launched a DDoS attack, TalkTalk's servers crashed, and the attackers appeared to have used the opportunity to exfiltrate a vast quantity of data. Customers were alarmed to hear that names, addresses and dates of birth had been seized, as well as credit-card and bank details. The theft potentially left them open to phishing attacks or identity theft. It soon emerged that TalkTalk had not encrypted confidential data (although this is not a legal requirement). Given that this was not the first time TalkTalk had been hacked, the statement by managing director Tristia Harrison sounded rather hollow: 'We would like to reassure you that we take any threat to the security of our customers' data very seriously.'[111] A few hours after the servers crashed, TalkTalk's CEO reportedly received a ransom note from the hackers, asking for £80,000 in Bitcoin.[112]

The hackers didn't receive any ransom. Just three days after the breach, the first arrest was made – a 15-year-old boy in Northern Ireland, followed shortly by the arrest of four other young men, two aged 16, one aged 18 and another aged 20.

On 2 November, TalkTalk announced that 1.2 million customer email addresses, names and phone numbers had been stolen (a few days later, it revised the estimate down to a far lower 150,000). The following day, an investigation by UK talk radio station Leading Britain's Conversation (LBC) reported that 2,500 customer accounts were available on the Darknet, each record with a price tag as low as 20p.[113] Stories emerged of customers who had had money stolen from their bank accounts but CEO Dido Harding claimed that she was 'not aware of anyone who has directly lost money as a direct consequence of the attack'.[114]

The hacking of TalkTalk by a group of lads cost the company around £60 million[115] to fix and greatly damaged its reputation. Shares in the company fell by a quarter in the wake of the cyberattack. Had TalkTalk been targeted by cybercriminals better able to profit from the venture, the situation could have been far graver. One year later, email giant Yahoo revealed that data from more than 1 billion user accounts had been compromised in 2013, apparently in a state-sponsored attack.[116] Such incidents make it clear that big companies need to do far more to guard their customers' data.

HIGH-LEVEL HACK

In 2015, 30-year-old Lauri Love from the UK was arrested under the Computer Misuse Act for hacking top-level US agencies including the army, the National Aeronautics and Space Administration (NASA) and the Federal Reserve. In December 2012, Love allegedly infiltrated the Federal Reserve computer system, placing hidden 'backdoors' so he could return later to steal data. Love considered defacing the site and publicizing the system users' passwords and phone numbers, saying in one chat to fellow hackers. 'You have no idea how much we can fuck with the US government if we wanted [sic] to.'[117] Accused of causing millions of dollars of damage over a year of hacking, he faced possible extradition to the United States.[118] The US government clearly wanted to focus on Love's cybercrime but the fact that a young hacker could easily access sensitive data has implications for public trust in the security of major government institutions.

EXPOSING CORRUPTION AND HUMAN RIGHTS ABUSES

Anonymous hacktivists and others take the law into their own hands to tackle what they perceive to be corrupt practice and expose human rights abuses. To them, it is perfectly legitimate to use illegal subversive methods to do this.

The HBGary Federal hack

Aaron Barr was the CEO of HBGary Federal, an up-and-coming US digital security company seeking big contracts with major corporations. He knew that Anonymous was a thorn in the side of the US government because of its support for WikiLeaks (see Political Activism below) and began to secretly track the group. Barr lurked in Anonymous chat rooms with the nickname AnonCog, and then CogAnon. He noted when people left chat rooms and moved over to Facebook. He friended people on Facebook who logged on just after signing off from an Anonymous chat room and attempted to match Anons with people using their real names on Facebook.[119]

Anonymous got wind of Barr's activities and decided to track him in return. It found that the HBGary Federal website was vulnerable to SQL injection – it was possible to smuggle commands into the database to gain access to the information.

Once inside the system, the hackers found the encrypted passwords of Barr and others. They uploaded them to the web forum Hashkiller.com, and within a couple of hours some helpful volunteers had cracked them. Barr's password, kibafo33,[120] was identical for his email, Twitter, Yahoo, Flickr, Facebook and World of Warcraft accounts – an incredibly basic error for a security expert, and one that allowed for maximum lulz. The Anons hacked all Barr's accounts, downloaded all his emails and decided to spy on him.

By January 2011 Barr was ready to dox a list of Anons and planned to sell their identities to the Federal Bureau of Investigation (FBI). Covertly reading the list, the Anons realized he had got most of the details wrong and was about to dox innocent people for profit. Not only that, but HBGary Federal was using illegal methods, employing Trojans, rootkits (software tools that allow an unauthorized user to take control of a computer system) and spyware to gain unlawful access to IT networks. The Anons noted the date Barr planned to meet with the FBI and prepared their attack for the preceding day.[121] Instead of being exposed, they would expose him.

ZERO-DAY EXPLOITS

Anonymous discovered that HBGary Federal had accumulated zero-day exploits for future use – these are software vulnerabilities unknown to the vendor that hackers can use before the vendor discovers it. Anons knew that the market for these vulnerabilities was extremely lucrative, with governments paying the highest prices. As Scottish journalist Ryan Gallagher explains, they can be 'weaponized and deployed aggressively for everything from government spying and corporate espionage to flat-out fraud'.[122]

Now the fun for Anonymous and hell for Barr began. On 6 February 2011, Anons locked Barr out of his accounts by changing his password and defaced his Twitter feed with offensive racist and homophobic messages – they weren't racist bigots but they wanted to make Barr look as bad as possible to subvert his authority. They revealed all Barr's personal details and invited people to call him. The Anons released all his emails on a WikiLeaks-type site called AnonLeaks for the whole world to view.

Taking control of HBGaryFederal's website took a little more effort. Anon Ops member Sabu contacted an HBGary IT admin, posing as Chief Technology Officer Greg Hoglund in a rush before a meeting and needing the user name and password to log in to the server and gain access to rootkit. com – the programming tools for accessing the computer system.[123] It was a classic case of using social engineering to gain key security information. Once they controlled rootkit. com, Sabu and fellow Anon Kayla deleted the site contents, left a blank page with the words 'Greg Hoglund = Owned' and replaced the HBGaryFederal.com home page with a white screen displaying the Anonymous logo.[124] Barr's career at HBGary was well and truly over. Anonymous believed this attack on HBGary was morally justified, although it was clearly illegal.

Operation Anti-Sec, 2011

For Anons, the anti-security movement was a fight to expose the corruption of the white-hat security industry, which took large sums of money from companies but did not bring them genuine security. As a post from June 2011 stated, 'Your hat can be white, gray, or black, your skin and race are not important. If you're aware of the corruption, expose it now, in the name of Anti-Security.'[125] Operation Anti-Sec also vowed to expose intelligence companies that secretly monitored activist groups.

In December, Anonymous hacked the Austin, Texas-based company Stratfor, a global intelligence service involved in monitoring activists such as the Yes Men, who worked to raise awareness of the 1984 Bhopal chemical factory disaster, one of the worst industrial accidents in the world.[126] Hackers stole 60,000 credit-card numbers and records for 860,000 clients, staff emails and financial data. The Anons claimed they had used the credit cards to donate money to charities, including Greenpeace, the American Red Cross, Amnesty International, the Bradley Manning Support Organization and the American Civil Liberties Union (ACLU) as Robin-Hood-style Christmas presents in the festive month – but most of the cards didn't work.[127] And the FBI counter-claimed that US $700,000 (about £500,000) had been used for fraud. The FBI was soon able to arrest Sup_g, the hacker who'd broken into Stratfor – 27-year-old political activist Jeremy Hammond. He was handed down a tough sentence: a decade in jail for computer fraud. As Hammond commented, '[The prosecutors] have made it clear they are trying to send a message to others who come after me.'[128] Although illegal and heavily punished, the Anti-Sec attacks dramatically demonstrated shortcomings in Internet security. Anonymous and similar groups hacked for the publicity rather than for financial gain but they showed how easy it was for black-hat hackers to steal and sell data – a sobering message for governments and companies.

Edward Snowden: exposing secret surveillance

In 2013, US National Security Agency (NSA) subcontractor Edward Snowden gave up his highly paid job, beautiful girlfriend, idyllic lifestyle in Hawaii and his freedom after discovering his country's undeclared draconian surveillance programme. He leaked confidential documents that showed that the NSA – tasked with gathering foreign intelligence – was carrying out widespread domestic surveillance of American citizens. The Stellar Wind operation stored American data, which tech giants were forced to hand over. Ordinary Internet users were surveilled, but the government focused particularly on Muslims, environmentalists and hacktivists.[129] It also spied on 38 embassies and hacked the Qatar-based Arabic TV station Al Jazeera. To do this, the NSA was tapping seabed Internet cables, installing 'backdoors' into company servers so it could spy whenever it wished to, and working to crack encryption.[130] Snowden revealed that intelligence agencies were recording encrypted Internet traffic, so users could no longer rely on Secure Sockets Layer (SSL) technology to protect sensitive data.[131] He showed that from 2011, British security service Government Communications Headquarters (GCHQ) launched DDoS attacks against Anonymous, named Op WEALTH and Rolling Thunder.[132]

Copying top-secret documents was obviously illegal, but Snowden believed it was ethically right to expose the British government's covert use of illegal DDoS attacks. The British government was not condemned for its action yet Chris Weatherhead, known as 'nerdo', was arrested for participating in Operation Payback (see Political Activism below). He didn't take part in a DDoS attack but ran the Internet Relay

In 2016, Academy Award-winning film director Oliver Stone released a movie about Edward Snowden entitled Snowden. Talking to the director via a webcam from Russia, Snowden revealed that his life there was 'surprisingly free' but he regrets that he still cannot come home to the USA.

Chat (IRC) server where Anonymous actions were discussed. Outraged, he exclaimed: 'My Government used a DDoS attack against servers I owned, and then convicted me of conducting DDoS attacks. Seriously what the fucking fuck.'[133] Put more politely, it's an example of double standards.

Edward Snowden and others who reveal confidential data believe they are doing the right thing by uncovering government abuse of power. Yet their actions could compromise the security of the people whose details they have revealed. More significantly, governments believe it is necessary to carry out widespread surveillance to monitor would-be terrorists and foil their plans before they come to bloody fruition. They argue that the loss of individual privacy is the price we have to pay for the protection of the entire population. Whistleblowers therefore deserve to be punished for threatening the safety of the majority.

Justice for rape and abuse victims

Taking up another area of human rights, Anonymous has stepped in to subvert the US judicial system, believing it was failing rape and abuse victims. Anons became involved in the Steubenville case of 2012. High-school football-team members in Steubenville, Ohio, had raped a classmate who'd passed out, photographed her and then boasted about the crime on social media, joking that 'They peed on her. That's how you know she's dead, because someone pissed on her.'[134] She was not in fact killed. Angry about the lack of coverage of the shocking case in this town where football players were treated like royalty, Michelle McKee, herself a victim of sexual abuse, contacted Anonymous. Anons Deric Lostutter and Noah McHugh decided to act. McHugh hacked the school sports web portal, posted incriminating tweets and threatened to release the personal details of the entire team unless the perpetrators apologized to the girl.[135] Anonymous remained involved with the case until two teenage boys were found guilty of rape in March 2013, receiving sentences of one and two years in youth prisons. Lostutter and McHugh were themselves arrested for hacking and faced longer terms than the rapists.[136] The participation of Anons sparked controversy – were they shaming wrongdoers and aiding the judicial process or unaccountable vigilantes with undue influence on the justice system?[137]

Anonymous continued to take on a variety of campaigns highlighting the failure of the authorities to tackle human rights abuses, including Operation Death Eaters against child sex trafficking and the covering up of paedophilia, and OpFerguson, after the police killing of 18-year-old African American Michael Brown in 2014. Anonymous's actions remain varied, but are always motivated by a sense of outrage at the authorities and the challenge of undermining them.

POLITICAL ACTIVISM

From late 2010, Anons turned their hand to political activism to defend WikiLeaks and assist activists in the Arab Spring uprisings.

The WikiLeaks revelations

'Information, we say, sets us free. But who charts the boundaries between what may safely be deemed free and what must be wrenched from the jaws of officialdom? The plain fact is that free means really free: and Assange helped set that benchmark.' Peter Preston, columnist and former editor of The *Guardian*.[138]

Wikileaks continues to disclose high-level confidential materials; in July 2016, a searchable archive of more than 30,000 emails sent to and from the US Democratic Party presidential nominee Hillary Clinton was made available.

Intelligence analyst Private Bradley Manning of the US Army risked his career and freedom to leak 250,000 secret US diplomatic cables to Julian Assange, founder of WikiLeaks.

Manning's finds included reports describing 'friendly fire' incidents and the accidental killing of civilians in Afghanistan and Iraq. Julian Assange was particularly struck by a disturbing video of a Baghdad air strike in which two Reuters journalists were killed and two children injured. When the pilot heard on the radio that two children had been hurt, he callously commented, 'Well, it's their [the Iraqis'] fault for bringing their kids into a battle.' The children belonged to a van driver who had tried to rescue one of the journalists. Twelve people died during the encounter.[139] Assange meticulously edited this video of what he perceived as the blatant abuse of state power, entitling it 'Collateral Murder' – and released it to the world. He made his mark. Hoping to achieve maximum publicity for the goldmine of confidential material in the cables, he worked with five internationally respected newspapers: *The New York Times*, the *Guardian, Le Monde, El País* and *Der Spiegel*. Journalists spent months making sense of the leaked materials and sensitively redacting them to avoid revealing the identities of people who could be endangered as a result. From 28 November 2010, the five newspapers ran a series of sensational articles, analysing the most significant revelations.

SAVING OR ENDANGERING LIVES?

Assange argued that 'the great thrust of our work is to save lives ... we aim to limit the hunger for killings, skirmishes and invasions, as well as to limit the effectiveness of the lies that support them.'[140] However, the US government accused Assange of endangering lives by revealing confidential data about its military operations and dealings around the globe.

Operation Payback

Incensed by this release of confidential information, the US government immediately put pressure on major corporations to stop providing essential support to WikiLeaks. As a result, PayPal, Visa and the Swiss bank Postfinance withdrew their services from the whistleblowing site so that it could no longer take donations. In response, Anonymous launched Operation Payback against PayPal and Visa, using illegal DDoS and botnet attacks (see panel overleaf). Willing participants downloaded Low Orbit Ion Cannon (LOIC) software, which enabled them to join in DDoS attacks. The PayPal attack was planned for 8 December 2010. Twitter and 4chan users frantically posted FIRE FIRE FIRE!, and about 4,500 LOIC users pressed the big red button marked 'IMMA CHARGIN MAH LAZER' to launch their attack. But nothing much happened. The site only crashed when a couple of botnets joined the attack, with the mighty power of over 30,000 zombie computers.[141] Yet the Anonymous idea of the 'hive mind' – thousands of like-minded individuals working as one – was a strong motivating factor in the attack and may have persuaded botnet masters Civil and Switch to participate. Certainly, the myth of the hive mind was perpetuated to keep up morale so individuals could feel they had contributed to the attack and would continue their involvement in Anonymous campaigns.[142]

DDOS ATTACKS AND BOTNETS

In a DDoS attack, a vast number of computers try to access the same website at the same time. LOIC allows people to take part by entering the target IP address and directing their computer to send requests to the site.[143] The site cannot cope with the quantity of requests and it crashes. To create a botnet – a zombie army of computers – a hacker sends a Trojan to a large number of computer users, which they unwittingly download by clicking on a link or attachment. When the botnet master decides to activate the 'soldiers', he or she sends a command to all of the infected computers. The botnets may be used to direct traffic to a particular site in a DDoS attack or used to send out spam.[144] Botnet masters with many thousands of zombie computers in their army will hire out their botnet to others to use.

Experienced Anons knew that using LOIC was illegal but considered it morally acceptable. To them, it was hypocritical to argue that attacking PayPal and credit-card companies over their denial of service to WikiLeaks was wrong while far-right extremists could donate legally to racist organizations such as the Ku Klux Klan through those services.[145] Anons were led to believe it was safe to use LOIC because so many of them took part that it would be impossible to track them all down.[146] As it turned out, LOIC did not hide users' IP addresses, and many Anons were subsequently arrested.

The Arab Spring

Around the time of Operation Payback, Arab activists, with the support of Anonymous, took to cyberspace to subvert trust

Hosni Mubarak resigned as the President of Egypt in February 2011 and the military took control. Protests against military rule followed; this protest in Cairo's Tahrir Square took place in December 2011.

in governments that they believed were losing their legitimacy. In another case of legitimacy versus legality, hactivists defended the right to use illegal methods to counter illegitimate power.

In spring 2011, subversive movements against longstanding authoritarian regimes erupted around the Arab world – in Tunisia, Egypt, Libya and Yemen. People expressed their desire for regime change on Facebook and Twitter, engendering a sense that so many citizens were angry that the government could no longer ignore their protests. The numbers involved helped to undermine trust in the strength of the state. Once the movements had achieved momentum online, protesters shifted from virtual subversion to street demonstrations, not knowing whether their discontent could be successfully transferred. As Egyptian activist Wael Ghonim wrote in his book *Revolution 2.0*, on 25 January 2011 protesters called a public protest in Tahrir Square, central Cairo: 'We could not believe our eyes. I began tweeting like a madman on my personal account, urging everyone to come out and join the protest.'[147] Once the movement had come out on to the streets, it went beyond the subversive stage and developed into a full-blown uprising.

Although using Facebook and Twitter was not illegal, the explosion of online opposition presented a challenge to the Arab governments. They responded by clamping down on the Internet. In January 2011 Hosni Mubarak's government in Egypt censored Facebook and Twitter and spied on people online. It shut down the Internet completely on 28 January.[148] At the same time, the Tunisian government hacked people's Facebook and email logins and passwords through phishing attacks to spy on them. It then blocked all Internet requests from outside Tunisia.

Anonymous worked alongside activists in Tunisia and Egypt to build the protests and retaliate against their governments. Gabriella Coleman developed extensive contact with members of Anonymous and in *Hacker, Hoaxer, Whistleblower, Spy* she documents many instances of how protesters inside and outside Arab countries collaborated successfully. This is one example from Tunisia.

Operation Tunisia

In November 2010, WikiLeaks released Tunisia-specific cables illustrating the corruption of President Ben Ali to independent collective blog Nawaat in Tunisia. The cables showed that while the majority of the population barely survived in poverty, Ben Ali's family lived opulently; one dinner included 'perhaps a dozen dishes, including fish, steak, turkey, octopus, fish couscous and much more' – even the family pet tiger Pasha ate four chickens a day.[149] Details like these infuriated the population. Yet the international mainstream media, with the exception of Qatar-based Al Jazeera, failed to cover the rapidly growing forces for change in the Middle East. In January 2011, Anonymous wrote a typically strident letter to journalists demanding coverage.[150]

At the start of 2011, Tunisian activist Slim Amamou asked Anonymous to help publicize the campaign to subvert his government, and #OpTunisia was born.[151] After the government cut off Tunisia's Internet links with the outside world, Anonymous activist Sabu asked for a volunteer inside Tunisia to facilitate a cyberattack on its institutions. A Tunisian man courageously volunteered. By controlling the volunteer's computer remotely, Sabu brought down two servers, which took the whole Tunisian government offline.[152] Anonymous also launched DDoS attacks on the Tunisian prime minister and the stock market, bringing down any .tn sites it could.[153] In #Opdefacetunisia, Anonymous sent a direct message to the government, berating its abuse of the Tunisian people.

Anonymous activists in #OpTunisia were working round the clock, but the Tunisians were risking their freedom. The volunteer who worked with Sabu on the cyberattack was subsequently arrested, and Amamou was also arrested and imprisoned for communicating and passing software between Tunisia, Anonymous and the outside world. An Anon known as tflow (later discovered to be 16-year-old British Iraqi Mustafa al-Bassam) came up with a brilliant idea. He wrote an anti-phishing script to stop the Tunisian government from hacking into people's communications, and thousands downloaded it to protect their privacy when organizing protests.[154] When Ben Ali stepped down on 14 January 2011, it was clear that online subversion had contributed to the ending of 23 years of repressive dictatorship.

CLAMPDOWN

Law enforcement authorities take a dim view of the use of illegal tactics in cyberspace regardless of the intentions of the attackers. The penalties meted out for cybercrime have been exceedingly high, especially in the United States, where long prison terms and huge fines are common. In the United States it is legal to use entrapment to catch cybercriminals, taking advantage of anonymity to pose as members of their organizations and covertly obtain information in order to arrest and convict them.

Back in 2010, most Anons were insufficiently careful about their own security when they taunted powerful finance corporations including PayPal and Visa; the police were able to trace people who'd used LOIC. Arrested for the DDoS attacks on PayPal, the 'PayPal14' escaped jail but landed heavy fines.[155]

THE RIGHT TO PROTEST

One of the few women arrested for involvement in the DDoS attacks against Visa was the troll Mercedes Haefer, who had joined Anonymous aged 19 in 2010 and claimed in her defence that protesting against Visa was a 'right': 'It wasn't about supporting Assange. It was about supporting freedom of speech and government transparency.'[156]

In 2011, truck driver Eric J. Rosol ran a DDoS tool against Kansas company Koch Industries website for 60 seconds in protest against the Koch brothers' role in supporting the Republican-led Wisconsin state, which was trying to restrict the power of many public-sector trade unions.[157] The operation caused financial losses of less than US $5,000 (about £3,500) but the Kansas court ordered Rosol to pay Koch Industries a disproportionate restitution of US $183,000 (about £129,700).[158]

On the other side of the Atlantic, in Ireland in 2011, young Anons Donncha O'Cearbhaill and Darren Martyn hacked and defaced the websites of Fine Gael, one of the country's major political parties. At their trial in 2013, the judge called their action 'a stunt to embarrass a political party rather than to disclose data to the public at large' and although they caused no lasting damage, the judge fined the young men €5,000 Euros (£3,900) each for their subversive act.[159]

In January 2015, US journalist Barrett Brown was handed down a stiff sentence for involvement in the Stratfor hack (see Operation Anti-Sec, 2011, above). Brown was no hacker and stole nothing, although he helped to develop Anonymous's strategy at the time and shared the group's links. For this, he was punished with almost five years in jail and a restitution fine of nearly US $1 million (£710,000) payable to Stratfor. The case sent a clear message to other journalists to avoid getting involved with subversive activity. Scared off, US journalist Quinn Norton subsequently said she would no longer report on security breaches, infosecurity or hacking.[160]

DDoS strikes and defacements by hackers undoubtedly incur costs for the victims, who have to fix their sites quickly and buy DDoS protection; their reputation may be damaged, too. But the attacks do not damage internal websites. Nevertheless, the punishments meted out are frequently harsh in relation to real-life crimes.[161] Involvement in a small operation can lead to a criminal conviction, and a lifetime of debt and difficulty securing employment.[162]

ENTRAPMENT

And what about the issue of double standards? Law enforcers may adopt the same methods as criminals, using DDoS attacks, hacking, malware and entrapment.

In June 2011, Sabu – Hector Xavier Monsegur, one of the core HBGary hackers – was arrested and forced to work for the FBI. Refusal would have meant going straight to jail, leaving behind two dependent cousins, whereas compliance with the FBI would lead to a more lenient sentence. Sabu became a key informant. Thus the FBI knew about the Stratfor hack (see above), and Sabu was permitted to break computer-crime laws so that law enforcers could pursue the perpetrator Jeremy Hammond and other Anons. Sabu fed Hammond lists of vulnerable targets, and Hammond broke in and handed the information to Sabu – even including hacks of foreign governments.[163] After Hammond's incarceration, Anons expressed their anger about entrapment through @YourAnonNews: 'Jeremy Hammond is serving a ten-year sentence for hacks that Sabu (working for the feds) told him to do. When will the feds go to prison?'[164]

SUBVERSION VERSUS THE LAW

Online subversion takes a variety of forms. Some actions undermine trust in companies. Hackers subvert devices they have bought to free them from the pre-loaded OS and mould them to their own designs, sharing the knowledge with others; it is hard for companies to prevent this. Highly skilled hackers attack major companies, apparently with ease, either just because they can or to expose corruption in the security industry – in the latter case, they believe they have a moral motive for breaking the law.

Those who reveal human rights abuses and government secrets also feel they occupy the moral high ground; their methods are illegal, but they believe their cause is legitimate. Edward Snowden's revelations showed the world the extent to which governments spy on their populations. Such hacktivists jeopardize their own liberty in the cause of information freedom. Online subversion can also play a direct role in political change in the real world, as demonstrated during the Arab Spring. Yet governments counter that releasing confidential information endangers the people exposed and weakens the fight against terrorism.

Computer hacker Hector Monsegur directed hundreds of cyber attacks on corporations and foreign governments before turning FBI informant.

The authorities have the law on their side but they sometimes adopt the same illegitimate tactics as their opponents. They have launched DDoS attacks, hacked the sites of suspected subversives and imposed heavy punishments on those convicted of cybercrime. Yet the hacker group Anonymous survives and thrives; as Anons say, 'you can't kill an idea'.

To avoid detection, activists have become more security conscious. In 2014, 'PhineasFisher' hacked into British-German surveillance company Gamma International and released evidence that it sold spyware software FinFisher to repressive governments[165], including Bahrain, which used it to monitor activists.[166] PhineasFisher posted the data on Twitter and Reddit and promptly disappeared. He re-emerged the following year to breach Hacking Team, an Italian surveillance company legally selling malware to governments that do not have the capacity to develop their own.[167] To promote his techniques, PhineasFisher published a guide for hackers: *Hack Back! A DIY Guide for Those Without the Patience to Wait for Whistleblowers*. Anons have certainly become more cautious. Whereas formerly they kept the same nickname, which allowed them to build up a reputation within the community, they now constantly change nicknames to make it harder for law enforcers or enemies to dox them. Just as with fraud, whatever anti-hacking innovations are introduced, hackers will find a way round them – and they even relish the challenge.

CHAPTER 5

CYBERESPIONAGE, SABOTAGE AND TERRORISM

On 23 December 2015, a power outage hit eastern Ukraine. In the freezing weather, people were left without electricity for up to six hours. Ukrainians were quick to accuse Russia of cybersabotage. An investigation indicated that there had indeed been a cyberattack by BlackEnergy malware from Russia, although it was unlikely that this had caused the power outage. It did however permit the attackers to hack into the SCADA production system, the computer systems that control plant operations and oil production in oil and gas fields, and infect workstations with malware. To restore services, workers had to switch to manual mode.[168]

Just a few years ago, such attacks were almost unheard of. Every year, the United States undertakes a Worldwide Threat Assessment. Cyberattacks didn't even make it on to the list until 2011. From 2013, they were listed as the top threat.[169] They include espionage, sabotage and organizing terrorist actions – all infinitely easier and less risky for perpetrators online than on the ground. In the United States, a cyberattack is defined as an act of war – even though it may not involve real-life violence. But it depends who carries it out. Non-state actors can be prosecuted for cyber assaults, while states use the same methods for what they consider to be a legitimate purpose – the defence of the nation.

States tend to carry out more cyberespionage than sabotage. They hope to gain insider knowledge of what other governments are up to. Commercial espionage is also common – illegally extricating sensitive data from companies in competitor countries. The Internet has allowed intelligence agencies to exfiltrate data without the dangers involved in sending undercover agents into enemy territory to steal it. Thomas Rid, Professor of Security Studies at King's College, London, argues that espionage is less violent in cyberspace since there is no need for spies to extract information from people using the threat of force.[170]

Yet the traditional divide remains between technical, or signals intelligence (SIGINT) and human intelligence (HUMINT). SIGINT requires specialists in decryption and cryptanalysis (deciphering coded messages) who can locate the relevant data to steal. You also need HUMINT to make sense of the data. It's not possible to simply download information about complex industrial or political processes and use it – you need to understand it. Tacit knowledge is involved: the insights you gain only from practical experience. Take the example of baking a cake. You can read a recipe that provides detailed instructions. But certain aspects, such as creaming the butter and sugar to the right consistency, folding in the egg whites and whipping the cream to the right thickness, can only be done well with experience. It is hard to present such knowledge through language alone.[171]

Therefore HUMINT is also required. Intelligence agents still need to recruit trustworthy informants who have the necessary tacit knowledge to interpret and analyse exfiltrated data. Successful espionage requires a combination of signals and human intelligence.

Cybersabotage ranges from hijacking a government or company website and defacing it to protest its actions, to attacking a country's infrastructure. The latter is possible because computers control everything from the water and electricity supply to traffic lights, trains and cash machines. Damaging computer systems may not harm anyone, but strikes on infrastructure could potentially contaminate the drinking water supply, disable a nuclear power plant or disrupt air traffic control, with disastrous consequences. Armed forces could disable enemy radar stations and missile launchers. Cybersabotage has been carried out by nations against each other and by organizations opposed to a government.

Cyberterrorism is the use of the Internet to harm a nation's technological and economic infrastructure, cause public disturbances and kill.[172] Arguably, the most successful cyber-terrorist movement has been the so-called Islamic State (ISIS). It successfully utilized a double-edged strategy to create a state: on the one hand, disseminating enticing messages to recruit fighters and supporters; on the other, broadcasting images of extreme violence and brutality to terrorize the opposition into submission. ISIS coordinated the terrorist attacks in Paris of January and November 2015 through a suite of anonymous online tools, including browsers, email programs and instant messaging.

All kinds of cyberattack appear to be on the increase, with the most powerful states at the forefront, other countries running to catch up, and non-state actors also participating in the action. Governments attempt to catch cyber spies, but if they are in another country it's impossible to bring them to justice without an extradition agreement. Security organizations are on duty 24/7 warding off sabotage attacks, yet hackers can always find vulnerabilities and break into computer systems. To defend us from terrorist groups, governments try to beat them at their own game with psychological warfare. They insist on the ability to intercept our communications to track terror suspects, leading to a debate about people's right to privacy versus the protection of society from mass shootings and suicide bombings.

CYBERESPIONAGE

When governments (or the governments of allied countries) undertake cyberespionage, they do not necessarily believe that they are carrying out a crime. For example, in September 2012 Debora Plunkett, director of the information assurance directorate at the US National Security Agency (NSA), stated that nation states were using disruptive cyberespionage – but only mentioned enemies of the United States doing this, rather than its allies. In fact, as Thomas Rid points out, 'Western countries are leading the charge in cyberespionage.'[173] And less developed states have entered the fray. Cold War-style spying, worthy of a John le Carré novel, is reaching new heights with high-tech spying tools. It appears that the United States and Israel attacked Russia with Duqu 2.0, while Russian hacking group Dukes carried out cyberespionage against Western governments. The Chinese have proved adept at commercial espionage to copy Western technology.

Political espionage: Duqu 2.0 and Dukes

In 2015, the Russian cybersecurity company Kaspersky Lab revealed that it had fallen victim to a cyberattack by Duqu 2.0. It believed the culprits were those who had developed Duqu 1.0, the worm used in the Stuxnet attack on Iran (see Cybersabotage on page 100): the United States and Israel. Kaspersky Lab realized that the malware was a very advanced cyberweapon. It had used three extremely expensive zero-day exploits (see page 72) and barely left a trace. US security company Symantec reported that Duqu 2.0 was definitely linked to Duqu 1.0 and shared a lot of its code.[174] This attack by a nation state on the security industry created shockwaves in the cybersecurity world. Under President Vladimir Putin since 2000, Russia has risen to become an important world power again but has frequently fallen out with Western countries, especially over its foreign policy – in 2014, its seizure of Crimea in Ukraine became a major flashpoint. Amid high levels of tension between the United States and Russia, the USA apparently deemed it legitimate to infiltrate Kaspersky Lab.

And Russia was hacking back. In 2015, Finnish security company F-Secure reported that Russian hacking group Dukes had been carrying out cyberespionage attacks against Western governments on behalf of the Kremlin. The group had used malware against specific targets, including government ministries, think tanks and subcontractors, collecting intelligence to help the government to decide on its foreign and security policy. Dukes apparently also attacked the Commonwealth of Independent States (CIS), Asian, African and Middle Eastern governments, and Chechen groups. Infiltrating the targets with spear phishing (see page 35), this sophisticated malware was created for long-term cyberespionage

An Iranian technician working at the Uranium Conversion Facility near Isfahan, Iran. In 2012, after the Stuxnet attack on an Iranian nuclear plant was revealed, Iran attempted to retaliate with DDoS attacks on the websites of US banks, but its attack was nowhere near as powerful or successful as Stuxnet.

– it could modify itself to avoid exposure. If detected, it altered its attack tools. Nevertheless, sufficient evidence remained to allow investigators to trace the attack back to Russia.[175]

FLAME

Initially called Wiper, the Flame cyberespionage program operated in the Middle East for six years before its discovery in 2012.[176] The Washington Post claimed that Flame had been developed by the NSA, the Central Intelligence Agency (CIA) and Israel and aimed to gather information about Iran's nuclear programme for a future sabotage attack to slow down its efforts to build nuclear weapons. The newspaper called it 'among the most sophisticated and subversive pieces of malware to be exposed to date.'[177] Dressed up as a Microsoft update, the worm was targeted to specific machines. It included a listening device that hijacked the microphone to record audio; secretly shot pictures; took screenshots of apps; logged keyboard activity; recorded Skype calls; sent and received data through Bluetooth and exfiltrated stored documents.[178] A powerful weapon indeed.

Iran – Rocket Kitten

Much spied upon by Western governments, Iran has developed its own cyberespionage capabilities. In November 2015, US–Israeli security firm ClearSky[179] discovered Rocket Kitten, a hacker group that allegedly carried out cyberespionage in the Middle East, Europe and the United States and targeted Israeli scientists, diplomats, members of the Saudi royal family, NATO officials, Iranian dissidents and human rights activists.[180] Rocket Kitten used a classic phishing technique – it created a false webpage to gather information. The hackers also sent malware in email attachments and used social engineering to gain access to their victims' email and Facebook accounts. As more nations initiate cyberespionage, this kind of retaliatory spying is likely to proliferate.

Commercial espionage

Hacking for commercial advantage is another growth area. The Chinese government is notorious for it. In 2014, the FBI in Pittsburgh issued an indictment of the China People's Liberation Army for allegedly hacking into the networks of U.S. Steel, Alcoa, Allegheny Technologies (ATI), Westinghouse, the US subsidiary of solar-panel maker SolarWorld and the United Steelworkers union. The FBI accused the Chinese of accessing thousands of emails over several years, containing information useful to Chinese companies about business strategy and industrial design.

By 2010, fracking for natural shale gas had become a major industry in the United States. U.S. Steel sold specially constructed pipes with no vertical seams so they could withstand being pushed down deep underground during the extraction process. The company was furious to discover that Chinese state-owned businesses were exporting similar pipes to the United States at lower prices. Likewise, the Chinese had hacked SolarWorld and were found selling solar panels at reduced rates. The US retaliated by introducing sanctions against China.

The FBI indictment explained how the Chinese hackers had infiltrated the companies. They had used the common technique of sending convincing fake emails that appeared to come from colleagues but contained malware in links or attachments. It wasn't possible to find out where the malicious emails came from because the hackers sent them from hop points – intermediate computers that they controlled. The spies set up domain names and programmed the malware on the victims' computers to contact the hop points. They could change the computer addresses to which the domain names linked so that they were difficult to trace. To reduce the chance of detection, they conducted espionage during the day in Shanghai while it was night-time in Pittsburgh. In this way, the Chinese gleaned details of U.S. Steel and other businesses that allowed imitators to develop competing products.

Eventually, US investigators discovered that the espionage originated from a building in Shanghai and identified the individual agents. This was the first case brought by the United States against state-sponsored cyberespionage, but the FBI could not arrest the perpetrators because there was no extradition agreement between US and China.[181] This story demonstrates that the security systems of major companies were not fit for purpose. As *MIT Technology Review* correspondent David Talbot noted, 'The failure of the companies' supposed security technologies was stupefying.'[182] With the apparent ease of infiltration, more and more states are implementing commercial espionage. Although it involves illegal hacking, for which citizens can be prosecuted when they strike governments or companies, nations have little recourse against external attacks.

CYBERSABOTAGE

Frequently a long-term project, cybersabotage often covertly damages systems for several years before security researchers notice it. It may have a temporary effect on computer systems, as in the case of Shamoon (a virus discovered in 2012), or cause physical damage, as Stuxnet did. As for espionage, effective sabotage requires insider knowledge to understand how to compromise systems and sometimes human participation as well.

Stuxnet

At the Natanz nuclear enrichment plant in Iran in 2011, the accusations began to fly. A few of the machines were failing and no one knew why. The engineers began to blame each other, certain that they themselves had done nothing wrong. It was worrying and potentially dangerous. Should they shut the whole system down until they could uncover the problem? As it was later described in the *New York Times*, 'The intent was that the failures should make them feel they were stupid.'[183] Eventually, the engineers realized the plant was being sabotaged remotely.[184] How long had this being going on? And more importantly, who were these cyber criminals?

The full story did not emerge until 2012. The United States and Israel had designed a sophisticated cyberattack against Iran's nuclear enrichment programme at Natanz. Starting in 2005, the covert attack, code-named Olympic Games, aimed to undermine Iran's confidence in its ability to develop nuclear weapons.[185] The sabotage software used a worm written specially to attack an industrial control system that was not on the Internet. The challenge for the saboteurs was to get it across the 'air gap' that protected it from the outside world to its target. Siemens engineers were helping the Iranians; someone may have carried in Stuxnet on a thumb drive – either willingly or not. All the worm's functions were in the hardware that was smuggled in.[186]

The worm aimed to physically damage rotors, turbines

and centrifuges. But it worked stealthily, so the operators wouldn't realize. Evading anti-virus software, it provided fake readings from the system while it changed the controller code in the background. The attack required a large team of people, huge resources, expensive equipment and a lot of time. Stuxnet did not stop the Iranian nuclear programme but it certainly delayed it; according to a US study, it was set back by one to two years.[187]

Shamoon

Saudi energy company Saudi Aramco is the biggest oil company in the world, controlling the largest proven crude oil reserves. On 15 August 2012, when the business operators started work, they could not boot up their PCs. Malware, including a wiper, which became known as Shamoon, had penetrated the business network, spread through network connections and wiped the hard drives of 30,000 computers – three-quarters of the total.[188] It took nearly two weeks to get the network back online. Cleaning up after the attack disrupted business and harmed the company's reputation. However, the malware didn't reach the SCADA network that controlled production; it was not on the Internet. If this had happened, serious damage and loss of life could have resulted.[189]

The Cutting Sword of Justice, aligned with activists in the Arab Spring, claimed it had attacked Saudi Arabia for supporting the repression of the uprisings. It published thousands of IP addresses of infected PCs.[190] But later investigators, including General Keith B. Alexander, then director of the NSA, believed that the blame lay with Iran.[191]

Such sabotage of other countries' utilities is on the rise and the capabilities to inflict damage are growing as ever-

Saudi Aramco's natural gas liquids plant in the Empty Quarter, Saudi Arabia. In 2015, it was revealed that when the Shamoon hack was discovered, all the company's computers were unplugged from the Internet and Saudi Aramco did not go back online for five months.

more sophisticated techniques emerge. Advanced learning software weapons are being developed that can observe and evaluate the environment, analyse courses of action and make decisions.[192] As with cyberespionage, states justify the sabotage of other nations' infrastructure to protect their interests, although any non-state actor carrying out similar operations faces prosecution for cybercrime.

ORGANIZING TERRORISM IN CYBERSPACE

On 13 November 2015, gunmen and suicide bombers linked to Islamic State simultaneously attacked a large stadium, concert hall, restaurants and bars in Paris, killing 130 people and injuring hundreds of others. Paris chief prosecutor François Molins believed that three coordinated teams had organized the assault. One team failed to explode their suicide vests inside the stadium; had they done so, hundreds could have been killed. A second team fired on diners in a popular restaurant area. The Bataclan concert hall endured the deadliest attack when gunmen fired assault rifles into the crowd, killing 89 and leaving another 99 critically injured; afterwards, emergency workers waded through a sea of blood to reach the victims.[193]

The atrocities were undoubtedly organized online using encrypted digital communications. One gunman mistakenly discarded a mobile near the Bataclan theatre; geolocation services on the device allowed police to find one of the attackers' hide-outs.[194] ISIS has proved adept at working in this way, as Middle East expert Abdel Bari Atwan notes: 'Without digital technology it is highly unlikely that Islamic State would ever have come into existence, let alone been able to survive and expand.'[195] Terrorist actions planned online could potentially be more widespread and have a greater impact than ever before.

Propaganda and recruitment

Most people who are interested in ISIS tend to be in their late teens or early 20s and grew up using the Internet. ISIS recruits specialists in IT, online marketing and security to run its online operation. Propaganda and recruitment are particularly effective areas. Experts in Internet technology, jihadists use high-definition (HD) cameras and editing software to produce sophisticated videos and magazines to attract support.[196] Every fighter can tweet from the field and share images on Instagram and short films on JustPaste.it. ISIS messages and videos can be disseminated to millions via Facebook, Twitter accounts and groups on Ask.fm, while the creators of the material remain anonymous.[197] Retweeting and the expert use of hashtags allow the messages to spread far and wide. ISIS regularly hijacks Twitter storms, using high-trending hashtags in tweets that link to ISIS material. During the 2014 World Cup, it used the #WorldCup hashtag to show a photo of a decapitated head, with the message: "This is our football, it's made of skin #WorldCup."[198]

If ISIS is about to release an important video, such as the January 2016 video explaining why it committed the November 2015 Paris massacres,[199] operatives tweet that something significant is about to happen. Its supporters then set up duplicate accounts. As soon as they receive the link on JustPaste.it or another anonymous message board, they quickly upload and distribute the material, and archive it in the Cloud or on mirrored websites, before YouTube, Facebook and Twitter administrators notice it and delete the accounts that uploaded it.[200]

New ISIS members in Western countries are usually recruited online. An ISIS member will direct message (DM) a potential contact and if the individual shows interest, the pair switch to an anonymous encrypted communication platform such as WhatsApp, Kik or Skype.[201] It is very hard for police or families of potential recruits to trace such conversations.[202]

IMAGES OF ISLAMIC STATE

ISIS has several radio and TV stations and film production organizations that promote a vision of Islamic State as an attractive place, where all live happily together and it is normal to seek martyrdom for your faith. Social media messages display the lighter side of life. Women tweet about their clothes and cooking and display photos of their children dressed as jihadis holding machine-guns.[203] On Cats of Jihad, fighters post pictures of cats relaxing on guns.[204] Al-Hayat produces short films of the daily life of the mujahideen, playing with children and helping the elderly, while Al-Furqan broadcasts TV series about ISIS's actions, often including bloody images of executions.[205] In 2016, ISIS launched a satellite TV channel called Bein HD4, broadcasting news and reports from the frontlines to half a million people in Mosul, Iraq.[206]

ISIS's online campaign has frightened its enemies and facilitated its victories. In May 2014, ISIS released images and videos of suicide bombings and beheadings on social media. The following month, the Iraqi Army in Mosul, Iraq, surrendered to ISIS incredibly quickly; the fighters themselves could not believe how easy it had been.[207]

The Cyber caliphate, hacking and doxing

ISIS also attacks opposing governments through the Cyber Caliphate (CC), a division of black-hat hackers. In April 2015, following the Charlie Hebdo terror attacks in Paris in January, it struck French media outlet Tv5 Monde, knocking out the broadcasts of 11 TV stations for several hours; the Cyber Caliphate also published the names of French soldiers, threatening to kill them.[208] In September, the group claimed to have hacked US government websites and accessed the personal details of more than 1,400 military and government employees to make a 'kill list'. The United States denied this attack had occurred.[209]

ISIS has also proved adept at using Twitter and Facebook to

dox its enemies, including military personnel, politicians and journalists. In summer 2015, it arrested 30-year-old Kurdish woman Ruqia Hassan Mohammed for openly criticizing the ISIS regime in her hometown of Raqqa, Syria, on social media. Few dared to do this; ISIS made it clear it would tolerate no dissent. The militia killed Mohammed in September but did not inform her family. According to another anti-ISIS activist, they hacked her Facebook account and continued to operate it to flush out other opponents. It is believed that at least five of them were subsequently arrested. Mohammed's loved ones finally discovered she had been murdered in January 2016.[210]

Hacking can provide valuable sources of funding, too. ISIS noticed that many retailers in the West were still using Windows XP, which is so old that security updates are no longer provided. This made it easy to hack their accounts to steal credit-card details for charging their stored-value credit cards (see Covert cash transfer, pages 163–4).[211]

Anonymous takes up the challenge

Hactivist group Anonymous joined the war in cyberspace against the Cyber Caliphate following the Charlie Hebdo attacks of January 2015. After the Paris attacks of November, Anonymous again vowed it would take revenge on ISIS. Launching Op Paris, an Anonymous spokesperson threatened: 'Anonymous from all over the world will hunt you down. You should know that we will find you and we will not let you go. We will launch the biggest operation ever against you. Expect massive cyberattacks. War is declared. Get prepared. The French people are stronger than you and will come out of this atrocity even stronger.'[212]

Anonymous took down 20,000 ISIS Twitter accounts and

sabotaged its sites. With their typical humour, Anons Photoshopped ISIS photos, turning jihadists' heads into rubber ducks. Following the ISIS mass shooting at a gay club in Orlando, Florida in June 2016 that left 50 dead and 53 injured, hackers linked to Anonymous stepped up their efforts to hijack ISIS Twitter accounts. They replaced ISIS propaganda with rainbow flags, pro-LGBT messages, such as 'I'm gay and proud' and links to gay porn sites. [213] Yet ISIS has simply labelled Anons 'idiots' – their antics are a nuisance rather than a genuine threat. If Twitter accounts are compromised, ISIS simply opens new ones.

Some Anons began to investigate hitting ISIS's finances, discussing how they might steal their Bitcoin deposits, which would be far harder than taking down Twitter accounts. The battle in cyberspace goes on. It is clear that cyberterrorism and counterterrorism by hactivists will escalate; yet neither is likely to completely overcome the other.

COUNTERING CYBERATTACKS

It's not easy to catch the perpetrators of cyberespionage, sabotage and terrorism. They usually lurk behind hidden IP addresses and proxy servers – unless they intend to claim responsibility for their actions to make a political point.[214] A powerful country may feel it can attack with impunity because there is no body strong enough to punish it. The United States and Israel never officially accepted responsibility for Stuxnet, although it became apparent they were the culprits.

Catching the spies

If an individual spy from your own country is the guilty party, you have a chance of punishing them. In 2012, a dispute arose between the US green energy company AMSC and

Chinese wind-turbine manufacturer Sinovel. AMSC had come up with a design that allowed its turbines to continue operating even when there was a power outage. It provided Sinovel with a sample of the software to try out. AMSC later realized that Sinovel was still using the software after the trial period had expired. How was this possible? It turned out to be a case of industrial cyberespionage. An AMSC employee had hacked the sample software and removed the expiry date so that Sinovel could carry on using it without buying the full version – in return for handsome payments. The spy was caught and sent to prison.[215]

On the other hand, if a cyberattack is attributed to hackers in another country and there is no extradition agreement, as between China and the United States, it is not possible to bring foreign perpetrators to justice. The United States is trying to work with the Chinese government to reduce cyberespionage. In September 2015, US President Barack Obama got a commitment from Chinese President Xi Jinping that China would stop carrying out commercial cyberespionage, otherwise the United States would introduce sanctions against Chinese companies that benefited from the theft. Obama said, 'We have agreed that neither the US nor the Chinese government will conduct or knowingly support cyber-enabled theft of intellectual property, including trade secrets or other confidential business information for commercial advantage.'[216]

One year later, it appeared that the level of Chinese hacking had reduced dramatically, from 60 network compromises in February 2013 to fewer than 10 by May 2016. Yet the attacks may now be more sophisticated and carefully targeted. Also, it appears that China has switched to alternative targets; Kaspersky Labs reported an almost three-fold increase in Chinese attacks on Russian industries in the first seven months of 2016.[217]

Stopping the saboteurs

One method of defence against cybersabotage is to improve security within companies, organizations and governments. NATO operates the Cooperative Cyber Defence Centre of Excellence in Tallinn, Estonia. It's linked to other NATO teams around Europe. The NATO compound in Mons, Belgium, run by Head of NATO's Communications and Information Agency Ian West, discovers 250–350 potential cyberattacks against NATO every week and many more against member states. As West says, 'Every single day, we are operational, experiencing attacks and defending against them.'[218] Teams like West's recruit hackers, most of whom enjoyed cracking games as teenagers; some will even have been convicted for hacking. After training and qualifying as white-hat hackers, they spend their time scanning for new threats and working out how to counter them. In 2015, Patrik Maldre, junior research fellow at the International Centre for Defence and Security, Estonia, recommended that NATO members come together to strengthen collective security against intrusion from Russia-sponsored hackers.[219] At the Cyber Defence Centre in Tallinn, hackers in their early 20s take part in cyberwar games to test the robustness of NATO's defences. They engage in exercises to practise stopping sabotage.[220]

LOCKED SHIELDS

In January 2016, the Locked Shields cyberwar exercise took place. The imaginary country Berylia

Staff at the NATO Computer Incident Response Capability (NCIRC) centre at NATO's military headquarters in Mons, Belgium.

(rather similar to Estonia) had been hit by a cyber assault on its drone manufacturer. The anonymous attackers were probably linked to Berylia's enemy Crimsonia (very like Russia). They found the latest cyber weapons on the Darknet and fired them at competing NATO teams to see if they could disable them. NATO cybersecurity teams around Europe competed to defeat the aggressor as quickly as possible and rebuild their systems.[221]

Another way to reduce sabotage would be to fix the 'backdoors' in all computer systems that governments insist on so they can spy on their own populations. This would make it far harder for hackers to get in.[222] A more extreme option, suggested by CyLab co-director Professor Virgil Gligor, is to reverse the connectedness of our world: 'We made access to services and databases and connectivity so convenient that it is also convenient for our adversaries.'[223] Countries and companies could unplug their systems from the Internet to avoid hacking – although this wouldn't prevent an inside job like Stuxnet or AMSC above.

Fighting terrorism in cyberspace

Although fixing backdoors could reduce sabotage, it is precisely those backdoors that governments argue they need in the fight against terrorism. On 2 December 2015, a married couple, Syed Farook and Tashfeen Malik, targeted Farook's co-workers at a Department of Public Health training event in San Bernardino County, California. Donning ski masks and black clothes, they opened fire on the guests, firing up to 75 bullets before leaving three home-made pipe bombs and rushing out of the building and attempting to escape. The police killed both attackers in a shoot-out. The mass shooting left 14 dead and 22 seriously wounded – the worst terrorist action on US soil since the 2001 Twin Towers attacks.

Following the ferocious killings, two crushed mobile phones were discovered near the couple's home. The FBI became determined to access the data on Farook's iPhone to find out whether the pair were linked to ISIS. But it was locked with a passcode; 10 incorrect attempts at the passcode would erase all the data on the phone. The FBI requested that Apple write new code to unlock the phone, arguing that it was essential to weaken encryption in the interests of security. It said that law enforcers need backdoor access to the information on mobile devices to fight crime. But, standing up for individuals' right to privacy, Apple's CEO Tim Cook countered that strong encryption was necessary to scramble data so that only the intended recipient could read it. In the light of such requests from governments, tech companies might work to make their devices even more secure.[224] The case raises an important debate about the right of a government to compromise individuals' security in the wider interests of society to fight terrorism.

USING PSYOPS AGAINST ISIS

In the UK in 2015, the 77th Brigade was formed for 'non-lethal warfare', its mission to attempt to counter ISIS recruitment online. For this psychological operations unit, soldiers with journalism and social media skills were recruited to try to win over 'hearts and minds' from the radicals.[225] The French government set up a similar unit, which launched an online platform called Stop Jihadism. Borrowing the violent visual imagery of ISIS and French slang, it recites the recruiting arguments of the Cyber Caliphate but refutes them one by one. For example: 'They tell you: "Come start a family with one of our heroes." In reality: You will raise your children in war and terror.'[226] The counterterrorist units are using similar tactics to their opponents to try to beat them at their own game. Their task appears monumental.

As of early 2016, as these debates continued, anti-ISIS governments were not winning their struggle against the Cyber Caliphate. As Abdel Bari Atwan notes, 'The battle in cyber-space is not going the way of governments. It is one that Islamic State, and other outlaw agencies, can continue to dominate, so long as the world's most tech-savvy youth – who hold the key to the codes required for effective cyber-warfare – do not want to fight in the same trench as the authorities.'[227]

However the battle in cyberspace between terrorist groups and governments plays out, it remains the case that the roots of ISIS cyberterrorism lie in the political conflict in the Middle East. Only peaceful resolution in the real world, through traditional, face-to-face diplomatic negotiations, is likely to stop the violence.

Escalating threats

Cyberespionage, sabotage and terrorism are growing more common and increasingly sophisticated. Countries spy on each other to glean political intelligence, while the potential rewards of stealing trade secrets make commercial espionage highly lucrative. Stuxnet, the most famous cybersabotage plot in recent years, damaged Iran's Natanz nuclear plant and set back development plans by up to two years. Islamic State has proved to be effective at cyberterrorism; it has specifically recruited people with a high level of technical know-how who can cloak their identities yet disseminate their message widely and openly, and continue to operate even after sites are closed down.

Some efforts to reduce cyberespionage have been made, such as the bilateral agreement between the United States and China of 2015. But it remains hard to attribute attacks accurately to the perpetrator and, without extradition agreements, it is impossible to prosecute attackers from another country. Cybersabotage is on the increase and likely to become more serious; the major sabotage of a nation's infrastructure could cause widespread destruction. As pr0f, a hacker who broke into a Houston water plant in 2011 to show how easy it was, warned: 'Eventually, somebody will get access to a major system and people will be hurt. It's just a matter of time.'[228] Law enforcers and hacktivists are mounting propaganda operations against cyberterrorism and governments are seeking greater powers to monitor our communications to try to prevent real-world attacks. It is unlikely that efforts to clamp down on cyberattacks will be truly successful unless relationships between nations improve; cyberespionage, sabotage and terrorism are an extension of real-world tensions and cannot be solved separately.

THE DARKNET

CHAPTER 6

CYBERCRIME
ON THE DARKNET

'The Darknet is ... very romantic ... it's been demonized. There are bad things that happen there just like there are bad things that happen anywhere human beings congregate.' Alex Winter, director of *Deep Web*.[229]

In July 2015, the FBI proudly proclaimed the success of Operation Shrouded Horizon. Arresting 70 people, the Department of Justice called it 'the largest coordinated international law-enforcement effort ever directed at an online cybercriminal forum.'[230] Black-hat hackers on the vast cybercrime and black market site Darkode were accused of wire fraud (see Chapter 2), money laundering and conspiring to commit online scams on a vast scale. One individual was accused of stealing data from 20 million people. Darkode's masterminds thought they could get away with it because their servers were supposedly 'bulletproof' – offshore in safe havens such as the Seychelles. But although law enforcers had taken down Darkode, that wasn't the end of it. A couple of weeks later, Darkode's main admin, Sp3cial1st, popped up again. Apparently unconcerned, he posted that 'the forum will be back', regrouping on the Darknet and out of the reach of the tentacles of the law. Next time, it wouldn't be found.[231]

That's because it's easy to hide on the Internet. When you browse the web, you are merely scraping the tip of a phenomenal iceberg. You're on the surface web, and Google has only indexed about 4–16 percent of it. The iceberg is the Deep Web; the quantity of non-indexed websites is estimated to be 400–500 times greater than the number on the surface web.[232] The Deep Web is the 'largest expanding reservoir of fresh information on the Internet'.[233] And within it lies the Darknet.

DEEP WEB AND DARKNET

The Deep Web consists mostly of protected content, and the quality of the information is generally higher than on the surface web. The websites usually have a narrower focus but more in-depth content. Some public databases are part of the Deep Web because normal search engines cannot index them; the US Library of Congress is here, as are the Directory of Open Access Journals, Wolfram Alpha and Census.gov. Pay-to-use databases and subscription-only services are on the Deep Web, such as Netflix. So are private and password-protected data, including bank and PayPal accounts, and government records.[234] Information on social networks is found on the Deep Web, too, and is not accessible through search engines, as is Instant Messaging (IM) – a private chat space that is not archived. If you want to keep the details, you have to record them during the discussion.

Part of the Deep Web, the Darknet has entered mainstream consciousness in recent years. We witnessed the dramatic arrest of Ross Ulbricht in 2013, mastermind behind the Silk Road drugs market (see page 121), and the popular US political thriller *House of Cards* (from 2013) included a shadowy hacker who had been 'turned' and worked for the FBI. The Darknet is used for anonymous trade, webhosting and cryptocurrencies (see page 127), for private messaging and file sharing. It is a place of freedom from regulation. A large part of what happens here is criminal activity of grave concern to the government and the public; there are 'drug dealers, hackers, hitmen, hoaxers, human traffickers, pimps, child sexual abusers, identity thieves, money launderers, leakers, political extremists, vigilantes, terrorists, and spies'[235].

The Darknet is 'dark' because it's hidden but it isn't hard to find if you know where to look. You need to use the Tor browser, which protects your privacy and allows you to access the Deep Web.[236] Here you'll find a menu for Tor Hidden Services. The site owners hide their locations but need to advertise so people can find them. To do this, they create an introduction point with a public key, but users can't associate it with the hidden service's IP address. There is never any direct contact between the provider and the user's computer – communication is always routed via other IP addresses.[237]

It used to be difficult to navigate the Darknet sites but it's becoming easier. In 2014, a hacker created Grams, the first distributed search engine on the Darknet. It allows users to look for illegal goods across many hidden sites. It's even got an 'I'm Feeling Lucky' button. There are also wikis with lists of hidden sites, which you can browse by category, such as hacks, drugs or computer viruses.[238]

WHO SET UP TOR?
Originally developed by the US Navy in the mid-1990s,[239] the US State Department and Department of Defense provide 60 per cent of the funding for Tor because it is a secure network for government data and for dissidents in undemocratic countries.

The Darknet is a confusing mixture of positive and negative elements. In this chapter, we'll focus on some of the negative and ambiguous ones. On the Darknet markets, consumers can buy a smorgasbord of illegal goods and services, using cryptocurrencies such as Bitcoin to preserve their anonymity. Most popular is the drugs market. Some argue that while clearly illegal, buying drugs online is safer than on the streets, while the innovation of anonymous payment systems is useful for society – it's an important debate. But law enforcers don't accept this view of drugs sales. They infiltrate the Darknet to attempt to catch the online drugs barons as well as the illegal marketeers, sometimes adopting entrapment and hacking to do so.

One of the most worrying areas of the Darknet is the lucrative market for live child sexual abuse and degrading images, which cause lifelong trauma to the victims. Even the most ardent freedom of information activists believe such sites should be wiped off the web. Law enforcers attempt to remove them and are developing novel techniques to trace child abuse materials. Is it possible to stop the worst abuses of the Darknet while accepting that this secretive world is likely to grow increasingly significant?

SHOPPING THE DARK WAY

You don't have to be a hacker to buy or sell illegal goods on the Darknet. Once you've reached the Darknet via Tor, you'll find easy-to-navigate sites just like regular websites. The Darknet markets are a free-for-all for buying all kinds of illicit goods and services. Underage and want alcohol? No problem. Looking for a cheap gift that looks pricey? You'll find counterfeit art, books and e-gift cards. If you're hoping to enter the criminal underworld, you can purchase fake birth certificates and passports, along with stolen credit-card details and PIN numbers. You can employ hacking services or buy hacking software to have a go yourself. Want someone dead? Hitmen accept payment in Bitcoin and provide photographic evidence that they have carried out the dirty deed. An underground trade in human organs exists, and you can buy weapons; they come wrapped in shielded packages so they don't trigger X-ray machines during transit.[240] Human traffickers ply their nefarious trade here, too. US attorney and Darknet law enforcer David J. Hickton has called the Darknet 'the Wild West of the Internet'.[241]

By far the most popular Darknet market is in illegal drugs. A few large dealers and many moderately sized ones are here, and most can ship to all countries. On their user-friendly sites, you can search by category of drugs or look down the bestseller list to see what everyone else is buying. The online drugs market exploded in popularity after Silk Road came on the scene in 2010.

Silk Road

Ross Ulbricht from Austin, Texas, hadn't had much luck with his career. In 2009, he heard about the cryptocurrency Bitcoin[242] (see page 127) and came up with the brainwave of setting up a website where people could buy and sell what they liked, anonymously. He set his sights on the drugs trade.

To libertarian Ross, taking drugs was a personal choice – the government had no right to tell people what they could consume. He thought the government war on drugs was pointless and that technology could eliminate the street violence associated with the illegal drugs trade. Ulbricht wouldn't deal drugs himself but would facilitate the market.[243] No child sexual abuse images or trade in stolen goods would be allowed. Ulbricht adopted the nickname Dread Pirate Roberts, the fictional pirate in the novel *The Princess Bride*.

Modelled on Amazon and eBay but accessed through Tor Hidden Services, Silk Road – named after the historic trade routes between Europe and the Far East – went live in January 2011. After it got coverage in US media blog *Gawker* in June 2011, thousands signed up, and the profits began rolling in.[244] Unsurprisingly, cannabis was the most popular product.[245] The sellers on the site were anonymous but customers gave their real address and packages arrived through the regular post.[246] Consumer rights were key, with reviews of vendors and a customer service complaints system. Security was tight – customers paid anonymously using Bitcoin, and Silk Road got a cut of the sales. The venture was extraordinarily successful, and Ross became a multimillionaire. But his luck did not last (see Shutting down the dark markets, below).

Drugs: a burgeoning market

Other online drugs markets appeared, mimicking Silk Road. As on the surface net, successful Darknet sites have 'trust cues' – they are well designed and easy to navigate to give the user confidence. They have recognizable logos and branding, and glossy high-resolution images illustrate the products. Drugs sites compete to attract users with special

A supporter of Ross Ulbricht outside a Manhattan court on the first day of the drug lord's trial in January 2015. In May, Ulbricht was sentenced to life imprisonment for running the Silk Road online drugs market.

offers.[247] You can even buy your drugs ethically! James Martin, author of *Drugs on the Dark Net*, discovered that some vendors sell drugs that are fair trade, organic or sourced from a conflict-free area: 'We are a team of libertarian cocaine dealers. We never buy coke from cartels! We never buy coke from police! We help farmers from Peru, Bolivia and some chemistry students in Brazil, Paraguay and Argentina. We do fair trade!'[248]

Such marketing strategies imply the dealers believe social responsibility is important to the buyers.[249] But according to Darknet expert Jamie Bartlett, the main reason for the success of online drugs markets is good customer service.[250] The sites operate a refund policy and have a list of Terms and Conditions for both parties. So buyers are less likely to get ripped off online than on the streets.

PROFESSIONAL SERVICE

When Jamie Bartlett bought a small quantity of marijuana (for research purposes, naturally), he was impressed by the professionalism of the Darknet sites. After reading reviews on the Darknet forums, he opted to buy from Drugsheaven,[251] which had an average customer satisfaction rating of 4.85 – but has since been shut down.[252] One review said: 'First order was lost ... I got a reship and now im [sic] very happy ... Heaven is one of the best dealers on the road!!! Very friendly and good communication, too. I will be back soon ;-) 5/5' When Bartlett contacted the vendor personally about his order, he received a prompt and very polite response, and his drugs arrived in perfect condition.[253]

Safer than the streets?

However, some drugs sites are less reliable than others; fraudulent sites exist that simply take people's money. Illegal sites with anonymous buyers and sellers have no regulators and there is no one aggrieved customers can appeal to if things go wrong. Darknet market forums have developed to help customers to find out which sites are trustworthy. Buyers can check user rankings and reviews, and if they're dissatisfied with a purchase, they can click the 'report this product' button.[254] As on the surface net, people try to trick the review system, using fake accounts to post reviews and writing scathing reviews of their competitors. Yet there's a crucial difference between Darknet and surface-net sites. At any moment, a Darknet drugs site – however highly recommended – can be taken down by law enforcers, who seize customers' and vendors' Bitcoins. In 2014, Silk Road 2.0 was hacked and lost around US $2.5 million Bitcoins (£1.7 million).[255]

Despite the risks, more people are buying drugs online year on year. The 2016 Global Drug Survey showed that almost one in ten of the 100,000 participants had bought drugs from the Darknet at some time, with 5 per cent stating that they had not taken drugs before buying them through Darknet markets.[256] They found the Darknet cheaper, safer and more reliable than other places because of anonymity and experienced less violence and fewer threats than when buying drugs elsewhere. But in 2015, 28 per cent reported losing money because of theft, the seizure of drugs by the authorities or exit scams, where admins disappeared with the Bitcoins.[257]

Illegal drugs are now more widely available than ever. Greater usage creates more misery: increased costs to people's health; the associated crime, including burglary and robbery;

and damage to the economy. Yet buying drugs online reduces the risks of violence and harm associated with the street drug trade because there is a shorter supply chain to the customer, as there are no middlemen to deal with directly and fewer impurities in the drugs. So it's a mixed picture; drugs are more widely available but generally less dangerous for users.[258]

Prescription meds

Legal prescription drugs are also big business on the Darknet. Ross Whitaker in the United States explains how the high cost of medicines meant that he could not afford a new asthma inhaler for his wife Jackie. Even with his insurance policy, it would have cost a prohibitive US $300 (£215). In desperation, Jackie suggested he check the Darknet. He found a plethora of prescription medicines at knock-down prices, including the correct inhaler. But how could he be sure he was buying a trustworthy product? Street drugs expert Dr Fernando Caudevilla notes that generic brands from eastern Europe, India and Brazil are usually reliable but it is best to check the seller's reputation. Ross did this, and decided to take the plunge. He knew the transaction was illegal because he had no prescription. Nervously, he purchased Bitcoins face-to-face with cash from the company LocalBitcoins, transferred them to an online wallet and used the TAILS operating system from a flash drive so it would leave no trace on his computer (see page 153). He used public Wi-Fi and Tor to access the wallet and transfer the payment, and Pretty Good Privacy (PGP) to encrypt his name and address so they were visible only to the vendor. After a few anxious weeks, the inhaler arrived from an unknown foreign country in swathes of packaging: the correct product, in mint condition.[259]

CRYPTO-SHOPPER: BITCOIN

How can people shop anonymously on the Darknet without using a personal credit card? Innovative techniques have been developed for making payments and ensuring that transactions remain under the radar. Some of these security features could prove useful for mainstream financial transactions.

Bitcoin

Started in 2009, Bitcoin was the brainchild of Satoshi Nakamoto. Bitcoin is an online anonymous currency, with no independent value and no ties to any currency. Anyone can download a Bitcoin wallet – you buy Bitcoins through a currency exchange and use them to buy products or services on the Darknet and, increasingly, from some offline businesses. Satoshi placed a cap on the total number of Bitcoins that could be produced – 21 million. No central authority creates new ones; instead, they are 'mined' by powerful computers competing with each other to solve ever more complex mathematical problems.

For security, Satoshi established a distributed rather than central verification system. Transactions are collected in blocks: each block contains 10 minutes of transactions and is known as a blockchain. Everyone who has Bitcoin software has a copy of the entire blockchain record. They all have a record of how many Bitcoins each person has. This system prevents fraud because no single person can alter the blockchain record.

In 2010, Satoshi disappeared, in true Darknet style.[260] To this day, no one knows his or her true identity. But the currency continued: in 2012, the Bitcoin Foundation was set up to regulate it. By 2015, there were commonly 100,000

Bitcoin is of course a virtual currency, but in recent years physical Bitcoins have also been created, mostly as collectible items.

transactions per day.[261] Millions of pounds worth of Bitcoins are traded, out of the control of states; governments cannot regulate the market or collect any tax on the transactions.

Escrow

Ross Ulbricht enthusiastically adopted Bitcoin for the Silk Road. But how could he ensure that anonymous crooks actually paid each other? A cunning escrow system emerged. The buyer transferred money from their Silk Road wallet to an escrow, controlled by an admin. The vendor sent the order. When the customer received it, he told the admin, who released the money to the vendor. Although this improved security, both parties had to trust the website, which could be taken down by law enforcers at any moment.

After the Silk Road was shut down (see Shutting down the dark markets, below), multi-signature escrow was introduced. The site as well as the vendor or buyer had to approve the transaction so that no one person could sneak off with the Bitcoins. Once two out of the three parties had signed off with their PGP key (encrypted digital signature), the vendor received the money. To increase security further, buyers avoided transferring money to their Bitcoin accounts from a real-world bank account by using cash to buy Bitcoins. Bitcoin developed a tumbling service so that different users' Bitcoins were mixed together and then forwarded to the payee, making it impossible to connect the buyer to the vendor.

Dark Wallet

Things move quickly on the Darknet. As soon as major companies started sniffing around Bitcoin, dedicated financial libertarians felt it was going mainstream. Amir

Taaki, living in an autonomous hacker space in a community in Calafou, Spain, dreamt up the Dark Wallet, which would be even more anonymous and trustworthy.[262] Launched in 2014,[263] using Dark Wallet avoids the need to download Bitcoin software on a computer – you can use it directly from the browser. The blockchain queries are routed through an Obelisk server,[264] set up especially for Dark Wallet. It's an open-source code so people don't have to rely on blockchain data providers. The developers say of Obelisk, 'If you don't know what it is, you don't need it.'[265] As well as a multi-signature escrow and tumbling service, it uses stealth addresses. A new Bitcoin address is generated for each transaction so that it is standalone. No one can check a person's transaction history because there simply is no history.[266]

Force for good?

Amir Taaki believes Dark Wallet and other cryptographic tools are part of a political project to allow people to live more freely, diverting economic power away from states and leading to a more progressive society. Certainly, Dark Wallet can lead to some decentralization of economic activities, but it's hard to see how this will transform society. And if more people use cryptocurrencies, they avoid paying tax and duties, leading to a shortage of tax revenue for governments.[267] Also, Bitcoin and Dark Wallet are not illegal but they provide the perfect payment system for cybercriminals to cover up illegal transactions, launder money, and trade in counterfeit currency and fake documents. Thus cryptocurrencies have a mixed effect; as Jamie Bartlett notes, 'The dark net is not black and white: it is confusing shades of grey.'[268]

SHUTTING DOWN THE DARK MARKETS

As the dark markets have grown, so too have efforts to stop them. Law enforcers use a variety of methods to try to stop cybercrime on the Darknet, including entrapment, hacking and search engines that can trawl Darknet sites.

Entrapment

Unknown to Ross Ulbricht, busily building up his drugs empire, he was being tracked by an undercover FBI agent who had been buying drugs on the Silk Road to gather intelligence. Both signals intelligence (hacking) and human intelligence – entrapment (see page 88) – enabled the Feds to close in on him.

In 2012, FBI Special Agent Carl Mark Force IV laid his trap. Posing as a drug cartel owner from the Dominican Republic, 'Nob' Eladio Guzman, Force contacted Dread Pirate Roberts, explained how impressed he was with Silk Road and asked if he could buy the site. Ulbricht declined but he built up a relationship with his new friend over the coming months. Little did he know that he was allowing the FBI to gain intelligence about his drugs empire. In 2013, the Feds were able to arrest Green, a senior collaborator in Ulbricht's network. Ulbricht panicked; he was terrified that Green would leak vital information about his set-up. Taking a deeper plunge into the criminal underworld, he employed Nob as a contract killer to eliminate Green. Nob pretended to do this, provided a fake photo showing Green apparently dead, and was paid $40,000 (£28,400) for his efforts.

The breakthrough for the FBI came when Special Agent Chris Tarbell managed to uncover Silk Road's IP address. He had spotted a warning on Reddit that the Silk Road IP address was 'leaking' – other computers could see it. A user had informed Dread Pirate Roberts but he had let down his guard somewhat and ignored the warning. Tarbell threw inaccurate user names and passwords at the site so he could analyse the IP addresses that communicated back with his machine. He engineered it so he could see the true IP address and traced Ulbricht to his rented room in San Francisco. The police didn't ask him about Silk Road but searched his home and took a clutch of fake IDs as evidence. By now, Ulbricht was extremely stressed – a millionaire many times over, he was losing control, paying blackmail money to hackers to stop them DDoS-ing the site, keeping sensitive data on his computer and even writing a diary. It was an opsec (operational security) disaster waiting to happen. The Feds closed in on Ulbricht and arrested the 29-year-old in October 2013, as well as several other Silk Road admins. Evidence on Ulbricht's computer included a file called emergency.txt that was never used:

- Destroy laptop hard drive and hide/dispose

- Hide memory stick

- Go to end of train [perhaps to log on where it was unlikely there would be surveillance][269]

- Find place to live on craigslist for cash

- Create new identity (name, backstory)

But before he could act on the plan, the Feds were at his door.[270]

Law enforcers invest vast resources in tracking and stopping operations such as the Silk Road. But does shutting them make a difference? Vendors and buyers on the site lose their Bitcoins and key admins might be arrested. But the risks of closure inspire Darknet site owners to ever-greater innovation. They mirror their sites so they are easy to set up again elsewhere if shut down. Hydra-like, they simply reappear in other places. Is it possible for countries to work together to act more effectively to stop dark markets?

Tracking the Darknet

Law enforcement agencies have been working on how to access the Darknet and decrypt information. Software security firm Hacking Team has been selling its services to the FBI, which spent nearly US $775,000 (£551,000) on them in 2011–15.[271] Hacking Team claims its software allows you to see what the target is doing, even on the Darknet. But Hacking Team was itself hacked in July 2015 and its emails released. They showed the company was using its spyware to reveal the IP addresses of people using Tor. Just because you are using Tor does not mean you are a cybercriminal. Given that the US government helps to fund Tor, this means that one part of the administration is working to crack the system that another part of the government is funding!

On another tack, the US Department of Defense Advanced Research Projects Agency (DARPA) is working on accessing the Darknet via a search engine. DARPA's Dr Christopher White has created Memex, a search engine that can trawl the Deep Web and Darknet just as Google does the surface web. Various government agencies are working with DARPA to adapt Memex for their needs, for example, to hunt down human traffickers.[272] However, it has serious limitations; it can't search sites that are password-protected (as Darkode was) or those behind a paywall.[273]

Some experts have argued that it is necessary to focus on

'bad actors' rather than trying to stop the Darknet altogether.[274] This would require a broad, global strategy of prevention, detection and response, with countries working together to counter illicit uses of the Internet. But it is difficult to achieve international agreements on approaches; major powers Russia and China resist the development of an international consensus to work together against cybercrime. And states with poor regulation in the real world are unlikely and unable to take action to stop the Darknet.[275]

CHILD SEXUAL ABUSE AND THE FIGHT TO STOP IT

47 RULES OF THE INTERNET[276]

'35 If no porn is found at the moment, it will be made

36 There will always be even more fucked up shit than what you just saw'

On the Darknet, criminal gangs organize sexual abuse 'shows'. Paedophiles can connect to the live rape of children and can even 'rape on demand', messaging the attackers to carry out particular types of abuse while they watch. In one case discovered by police, viewers ordered a group of men to rape an eight-year-old girl.[277]

The arrival of the Internet led to an explosion of child sexual abuse. Much of it is on the surface web but hidden away. To avoid detection by law enforcers, abuse sites have become very sophisticated. Viewers might have to arrive at a site by going via other sites in a certain order to reach the link to the hidden version with the illegal material. Those who arrive at the site any other way see regular adult images.

Often, a link takes users to a 'cyber locker', a hacked website where illegal files are stored without the knowledge of the website owner. But child abuse materials are extremely easy to access through Tor Hidden Services – a few clicks and you are viewing illegal material.[278]

Is it possible for law enforcers to shut down child abuse sites on the surface web and Darknet and stop the material being recycled on new sites? Is it ethical to use illegal means for the legitimate purpose of eliminating abusive imagery? And if sites are taken down, how can law enforcers stop the perpetrators who are abusing the children in the first place and uploading the videos? There are many debates around this sensitive issue and no easy answers.

Explosion of online abuse

Selling access to child sexual abuse online is a highly profitable business. No one really knows the proportion of visits to the Darknet that are for viewing such material. Cybersecurity expert Gareth Owen's 2014 research showed that a high number of visits to the Darknet were to child abuse sites, but a number of experts queried his counting methods.[279] Evidence indicates that most viewers are men and often well educated. It appears that browsing behaviour can lead viewers to gradually view younger and younger children. In the UK, the legal age of consent is 16 but any sexual material showing under-18s is illegal. The most popular category of online porn is 'legal teen'. There's a lot of barely legal 'jailbait' porn – teens who could be underage but it is hard to tell exactly how old they are. Many viewers stick with jailbait porn, but some find themselves attracted to increasingly younger children. It's so easy to click from link to link and move from viewing teenagers to children.[280] Within the child abuse sites, some extreme categories exist – 'hurtcore' is child sexual abuse that involves violent physical assaults on children. A researcher for *Cracked* discovered a poll on 7axxn, a child abuse site with more than 90,000 users. Almost 40 per cent of respondents said they loved hurtcore, while nearly 20 per cent thought it was OK.[281]

And as we saw on page 16, Suler's Online Disinhibition Effect allows people to develop a different persona online. They may believe they are able to view child sexual abuse but that it is harmless because they would never commit such acts themselves. But in order to post the abuse online, real people are violating real children, and the demand for the material is growing. Can anything be done to stop this cybercrime?

Combating the abusers

One way to stem the tide of abusive images is to hunt for them and remove them from the Internet. Virtual Global Taskforce works internationally to combat online sexual exploitation. People can report abuse on the site. The Taskforce tries to build links between law enforcement agencies, non-governmental organizations and industries in different countries to identify children at risk and hold the perpetrators to account.

OPERATION ENDEAVOUR

The UK National Crime Agency, Australian Federal Police and US Immigration and Customs Enforcement jointly ran Operation Endeavour. In 2014, after two years of hard work, they nailed a criminal group that was organizing live streaming of on-demand child sexual abuse in the Philippines. It led to 29 arrests worldwide, including 11 of the organizers in the Philippines, and 15 children aged 6–15 were rescued.[282]

In the UK, the Internet Watch Foundation (IWF) scans for child sexual abuse on the surface web, usually on sites hosted in countries where the police do not check. It's a horrible job. To make sure they are prepared for it, potential recruits have to view the offending images, from the lowest level of obscenity to the most extreme, with a Level 5 rating. They have to decide if they are able to look at such material, day in, day out, in order to remove it from the Internet. Deputy CEO of the IWF Fred Langford remembers the last day of his trial week: 'As I cycled home, I had this Level 5 image going round and round in my head. I couldn't get rid of it.' Perhaps he couldn't do the job after all. But over the weekend, he decided he wanted to dedicate his efforts to stopping the abuse.[283]

The Darknet makes the job of the IWF difficult – it is extremely hard to trace material there. People upload content anonymously using Tor Hidden Services and encryption. Other users download and share it through peer-to-peer file-sharing, widening its distribution.[284] International cooperation is hindered by hostility between rival countries such as Russia and the United States – for example, some Russian webhosting companies have no rules about content, allow customers to remain anonymous and frequently ignore subpoena requests from other countries.

The hash list

In 2015, IWF announced a technological development. CEO Susie Hargreaves called it nothing less than a 'game changer' that will 'change how we find and remove criminal content forever – the IWF Hash List'.[285] Analysts hashed images of child sexual abuse found online, giving each image a digital fingerprint that would allow it to be identified. This allowed industry services such as Google, Microsoft, Twitter and Facebook to find and remove the images on the Internet. Different types of hashes were available; Microsoft's PhotoDNA hashes could identify images even if they had been altered, while the cryptographic hashes MD5 and SHA1 can find exact matches of the images. Usually, when services such as the IWF take down a site with child sexual abuse images, the owner simply sets up a new site elsewhere with the same images. But the hashing process means those images can always be identified.[286] This is an important innovation, although of course new images are constantly being produced.

Hacking the abusers

Since it is notoriously difficult to trace the distributors of child sexual abuse on the Darknet, the FBI has turned to illegal tactics to do so. In 2015, it launched a huge operation against what it believed to be one of the Darknet's largest child sexual abuse sites.

In August 2014, a bulletin board called Playpen was set up on the Darknet. It encouraged users to upload their child abuse images for distribution. Within a year, Playpen had 215,000 members, many of whom posted extreme images. Being on the Darknet, they thought they were safe from the prying eyes of law enforcers. But in January 2015, police seized the computer server running the site. The FBI took it over and ran the site from its own servers, using a hacking tool to infect users' computers. This allowed officers to identify around 1,300 IP addresses, leading to a huge number of arrests. As Joseph Cox of Motherboard noted, it was possibly the 'largest law enforcement hacking campaign to date'.[287]

Although successful, the operation raised legal and ethical questions.[288] The defending lawyer in the Playpen case questioned the mass use of illegal hacking. The FBI had used a network investigative technique (NIT). This captured the details of anyone who visited the home page and started to log in. The NIT discovered the user's IP address, operating system and MAC address (the computer's unique network address), and noted whether it had already logged that computer. Using one search warrant, it gained access to the details of around 1,300 users. Did the goal justify illegal hacking on such a wide scale?[289]

There's another vital issue. Jérémie Zimmermann points to the problem with simply taking down the abuse sites and arresting the viewers: it's saying, 'Oh, we just remove access to the bad stuff.' How do you reach the people responsible for committing the abuse and uploading images? Zimmermann argues that you need to get to the beginning of the chain: 'One thing to do is to ... disable the servers, to identify the people who uploaded the content in order to identify the people who produced the content, who abused the children in the first place. And whenever there is a ... commercial network and so on, go and arrest the people.'[290] He contends that you should leave the sites up while investigating them, otherwise you will never reach the biggest culprits – the producers.

THE BATTLE OVER THE DARKNET

The dark markets for illegal goods are growing in popularity, with a particular surge in drugs purchases on slick, professional-looking sites. Whenever sites like the Silk Road are taken down, fresh ones rapidly spring up to take their place. Law enforcers have had some notable successes in closing down Dark Markets – they shut down the notorious Silk Road in 2013 and Darkode in 2015, although replacement sites quickly emerged. They have developed Memex to search the Darknet and open it up to scrutiny.

Bitcoin and Dark Wallet are used on the Dark Markets to trade in illegal goods and for money laundering. It is likely that Bitcoin and other cryptocurrencies will be more and more widely used. Although they can be used to fund crime, it would be inadvisable to throw out the baby with the bathwater because there are many positive uses of cryptocurrency and, in particular, the blockchain technology behind it (see pages 146–7).

Particularly horrific and worrying is the explosion in child sexual abuse on the Darknet. International cooperation has enabled agencies from different countries to work together to take down child sexual abuse sites, the IWF Hash List makes it easier to identify abusive images, and the FBI hacked and destroyed Playpen in 2015. However, radical libertarians like the cypherpunks point out that you need to reach the perpetrators rather than merely censoring access to the sites and arresting viewers.

The campaign to stop child sexual abuse and other illicit online activities is hampered by a lack of international cooperation and the innovations of the cybercriminals that enable them to keep their operations running. There's an argument for encouraging nations to act together more effectively to fight the worst elements on the Darknet. But they will surely reappear elsewhere or dig deeper into an even darker and yet undiscovered region of the hidden web. The battle over the Wild West of the Internet has only just begun.

CHAPTER 7

THE DARKNET FOR ONLINE FREEDOM

Successful schoolgirl blogger Parisa Ahmadi writes about the films she loves, and her popular reviews are earning her decent money. For a young Afghan woman, having her own income is truly empowering. Like others in her situation, she has no bank account – Afghan girls rely on their fathers and brothers to look after the cash. But Ahmadi is lucky enough to be signed up with The Film Annex, which pays its contributors in Bitcoin. There's nowhere locally she can spend her income, but The Film Annex's e-commerce site allows her to buy gift cards from international companies like Amazon. The venture is giving Ahmadi her first taste of independence.[291]

We've explored nefarious criminal activity on the Darknet. But, as Darknet expert Jamie Bartlett says, 'For every destructive subculture I examined there are just as many that are positive, helpful and constructive.'[292] The Darknet is a place of privacy and safety for human rights and political activists, journalists, whistleblowers and people at the margins of society. There are no commercial adverts or pop-ups to distract you, and there is no censorship. You might think it's just authoritarian regimes like China that censor the Internet, but Western governments block many websites, too.

Owing to the need to maintain anonymity, the Darknet is by necessity a hive of creativity – people are continually exploring better ways to stay hidden and keep their interactions private. Bitcoin, the escrow system and blockchain technology are remarkable innovations that allow private, secure financial transactions over the Internet. A major impulse behind the move to the Darknet has been the growth of mass surveillance. Governments worldwide have turned to mass surveillance to monitor and control their populations, arguing it is essential to track criminals and prevent illegal activity. They are slurping data from every area of our lives – our Internet usage, location, phone calls and personal information. Some forms of communication are encrypted but law enforcers argue that since encryption can be used by criminals and terrorists, they should always have a 'backdoor' to be able to access communications. This allows them to track their opponents, such as Islamic State supporters. Yet it is precisely this surveillance that is attracting ever-greater numbers – mainstream as well as marginal-ized – to the underground world of the Darknet.

Communications remain secret on the Darknet, so users can avoid surveillance. People can operate incognito with anonymous browsers, and messaging and social media apps such as Twister or Jitsi, which encrypt data. Such privacy tools are constantly improving. Whistleblowers Chelsea (formerly Bradley) Manning and Edward Snowden and the whistleblowing site WikiLeaks used such tools to transfer and release confidential data. It was against the law, but they believed it was in the public interest and therefore legitimate. Activists in undemocratic countries such as China and Iran – and some even in democratic countries – have switched to the anonymous Tor browser to avoid the prying eyes of the state. However, the use of the Darknet by ISIS to organize its campaigns has reignited the debate about where the balance between mass surveillance and the individual's right to privacy should lie.

BITCOIN AND BLOCKCHAIN

'Bitcoin is breaking down the barriers of digital currency transactions and has the potential to transform the way we pay for goods and services around the world.'

Akif Khan, Chief Commercial Officer, Bitnet Technologies Ltd[293]

The digital currency Bitcoin (see pages 127–8) is secure, private and cheap for the vendor – there are no card-processing fees to pay. It provides total privacy and freedom from banks and governments. Since its inception on the Darknet in 2009, Bitcoin and a multitude of other cryptocurrencies have emerged. Bitcoin Foundation scientist Gavin Andresen described Bitcoin in a 2014 *Newsweek* interview as 'a just-plain-better, more efficient, less-subject-to-political-whims money. Not as an all-powerful black-market tool that will be used by anarchists to overthrow the System.'[294] And it is entering the mainstream.

Bitcoin is proving popular among the 'unbanked' – people like Ahmadi above who have no access to traditional banking. Its uptake is particularly high in Argentina, where the banking system is in disarray, people distrust financial institutions and only 33 per cent of the population have bank accounts anyway.[295] Although Bitcoin is volatile, fluctuating wildly in value, many Argentinians remember the hyperinflation in their country of the late 1980s; in comparison, Bitcoin appears relatively stable. To access the digital currency, the company BitPagos allows Argentinians to exchange dollars for Bitcoins. In many African countries, more people have phones than have bank accounts. The BitPesa service cuts out the need for banks, allowing people to transfer money through their mobile using Bitcoin. By 2016, BitPesa had spread to Kenya, Nigeria, Tanzania and Uganda.[296] For those transferring money across borders, using a cryptocurrency is economical. For example, using BitPesa allows businesses to transfer money between African countries and China without paying fees to exchange it through an intermediary currency.[297]

Bitcoin has potential in developed countries, too. In most Western countries, only a small percentage of people are unbanked, but the figure reaches 12 per cent in the United States. That's because banks refuse to service the poorest people. Bitcoin asks no questions and does not check people's credit history so it could give them access to a form of banking.[298] Cryptocurrency can also be useful for people with complex payment arrangements. Musicians have turned to Bitcoin to free themselves from the complexities of the music-industry payment system. Music royalties are mostly collected by Performance Rights Organizations (PRO), which handle the payments for a region. The payments are then transferred to the publisher, which passes them on to the artist. However, it is estimated that 20–50 per cent of the royalties never reach the musicians.[299] Using Bitcoin, payments can be automatically forwarded without going through a PRO. Since Bitcoins can be subdivided – right down to one hundred millionth of a Bitcoin (known as a 'satoshi'),[300] even tiny amounts can be transferred. Every single download can be paid for. Musician and composer Imogen Heap came up with the idea of Mycelia. A collective foundation called Spores hosts the creative content. Artists, known as 'mushrooms', contribute the content. They can control their input, what they charge for it and how they split the proceeds – in Bitcoin, naturally.[301]

BITCOIN BONUS

In December 2015, the artist Kyle Henry and his band Myco[302] released his single for free with a Bitcoin QR code on the cover so people could give tips. He received some positive comments:

'Thank you for doing this. Just listened to "Myceliated" and sent you a tip.'

'I sent you a tip to you 'cause I like your music (and Bitcoin).'

'Hey man great track I really like the lyrics and guitar also the album art is on point! I sent a little mbit over keep up the good work!'

Kyle Henry responded:

'The beauty of Bitcoin is that I have control of my own money and can deal directly with other people. It's more of a tip than purchasing the music. If they like the song they can tip ... if not they don't ... have to pay anything.'[303]

Blockchain

Blockchain technology started with Bitcoin on the Darknet, but has a variety of potential applications. It's a transaction database shared and controlled by all the participants, a shared public ledger. When a block of transactions is verified by the network, the ledger is altered, and everyone's version is changed simultaneously. Every block of transactions has a hash of the previous block, and adds to the chain of transactions.[304] No individual can go back and change a block in the chain to roll back their spends. There is one single, permanent public ledger, reducing the potential for fraud.[305]

Blockchain can be used to build applications that are not controlled by a big company. For example, Ethereum is a decentralized platform that runs applications using blockchain; everyone using an app has a copy of the entire blockchain record, and they can interact with each other without censorship or interference from a third party.[306] Such a system can be used as an escrow service for high-value items, such as artwork, allowing a vendor to trust a first-time customer.[307] In 2016, the British government began a trial using blockchain for welfare benefits. [308] Sir Mark Robert, the UK government's Chief Scientific Advisor, believes that distributed ledgers could be used for a variety of purposes as well as logging benefit payments, for example for saving and sharing medical records more securely. Blockchain could be used to record the ownership of high-value property such as houses. It might prove valuable for the distribution of aid, permitting the government to track where the money goes and prevent fraud. A limited number of people would have permission to make changes.[309]

In the business world, blockchain technology could potentially revolutionize transactions.[310] It could be adopted for contracts to transfer ownership, such as car-purchase agreements. Imagine that the remote digital key for opening a car is linked to the owner's account. If they miss one of their monthly payments, they won't be able to unlock their car, and software linked to their account forces them to pay a penalty before they can get behind the wheel again. This may sound draconian, but in countries with weak states, blockchain could avoid the need to deal with expensive lawyers or corrupt institutions.[311] These ideas haven't gone unnoticed by the big corporations; by 2015, most major banks in the United States had set up task forces to examine the possibilities of cryptocurrencies.

MUSE FOR MUSICIANS

As with Bitcoin, musicians have been quick to see the potential of blockchain. The MUSE blockchain platform has been developed especially for the music industry and can be used with cryptocurrency and regular money. MUSE utilizes a distributed ledger for music licensing, storing the copyright data in the blockchain and inputting licensing conditions, such as different fees for using the music in a film or a TV advert. It can split royalties between the people who share copyright. The system can also handle payments for music sales, merchandise and gig tickets.[312]

THE SURVEILLANCE SOCIETY

Government bulk surveillance and storage of citizens' communications is rapidly becoming the norm in countries at war, authoritarian nations such as China and Western democracies, too. It's legal but is it legitimate to spy on us so widely? Some people don't think so, which is why they are turning to the Darknet.

In 2011, German hackers and freedom of information activists in the Chaos Computer Club revealed that the German government was using a backdoor Trojan to spy on criminal suspects in Germany; the bugs became known as the *Bundestrojaner* – 'state Trojans'. The Trojans took screenshots of browser windows and Skype calls and recorded Voice Over Internet Protocol (VOIP) calls. The activists revealed that the Trojan itself had poor security so third parties could hack the sources for their own reprehensible reasons.[313] This domestic surveillance was halted in May 2015 but resumed in January 2016 in the wake of the terrorist atrocities in Paris of November 2015.[314]

Democratic governments such as Germany's argue that gathering information about their citizens is not the same as looking at it and that surveillance is vital to prevent terrorism and capture paedophiles. It appears hard to argue against fighting such serious menaces to society. But it's a grey area. The data can be kept indefinitely and even if it is encrypted, it could later be decoded with more advanced software.[315] As Chris Baraniuk of *Wired* notes: 'That data ... may get passed from regime to successive regime for years, with little or no public control over how it is used, regardless of who comes to power. It may also be vulnerable to exfiltration by enemy states, rogue groups or criminal hackers.'[316]

Sobering thoughts like these mean people may be careful about what they say on the surface net. On the Darknet, they can give free rein to their thoughts.

Whistleblowers: Manning and WikiLeaks

'Information sets us free. And it does so by allowing us to question the actions of those who would sooner we had no means to question them.'

Julian Assange, WikiLeaks[317]

The secrecy of the Darknet enabled Chelsea (formerly Bradley) Manning and Edward Snowden to make their astonishing revelations of human rights abuses.

Although in a low-level position, 22-year-old US Army intelligence analyst Manning, stationed in Iraq, had access to confidential sensitive material about the USA's military operations (see page 80). Manning was shocked that the American public did not know the details of the war that was being fought in their name and felt an urge to release the information. She later reflected: 'It's important that it gets out ... I feel for some bizarre reason. It might actually change something.'[318] Manning knew this action was illegal but she had high ethical standards and believed in freedom of information; to her, leaking the material was legitimate.[319]

Surprisingly, for an intelligence operation, security on the military base was lax. Bored soldiers transferred videos and music between computers on unmarked CDs.[320] Manning brought in her rewritable CD with Lady Gaga on it, and copied over the confidential documents. But what next?

On Thanksgiving 2009, WikiLeaks released more than half a million pager messages[321] sent on 11 September 2001, the day of the Twin Towers terrorist attacks on the United States. It was the first time Manning had heard of the little-known whistleblowing site. Relieved to have found the ideal vehicle for her leaks, Manning made contact with Julian Assange.

The WikiLeaks protocol

WikiLeaks had worked out how to operate on the Darknet. Its web-hosting company PRQ offered secrecy and a Virtual Private Network (VPN – using public wires, usually the Internet, to connect to a private network, employing encryption so the data can't be intercepted).[322] A client could connect to the PRQ server, and information could not be traced back to them.[323] The WikiLeaks laptops had military-grade encryption so even if somebody stole one, they could not read the data. The code to control the WikiLeaks site was stored on remote PCs, and the operatives had memorized the passwords. They used Skype for encrypted communication; the technology was Swedish rather than American and had no backdoor for eavesdroppers.[324] The Tor browser provided complete anonymity. WikiLeaks reassured potential whistleblowers: 'We keep no records as to where you uploaded from, your time zone, browser or even as to when your submission was made.'[325]

Secure transfer

Manning later described the secure connection that was apparently specially created so that she could leak her stash of documents to WikiLeaks. She'd downloaded the secret files using AES-256 (Advanced Encryption Standard) to encrypt them, uploaded them via a secure File Transfer Protocol (FTP) to a server and sent her encryption passcode separately via Tor.[326] Manning's technological know-how was faultless, but she was caught out through human error. Desperate to offload her anxiety about leaking confidential materials, she confessed to US hacker Adrian Lamo over the Internet, and Lamo promptly reported her to the authorities,

Wikileaks founder Julian Assange prepares to speak from the balcony of the Ecuadorian embassy in London where he has taken refuge since 2012.

believing soldiers' lives could be endangered by the release of the information.[327] Manning was immediately arrested.

Nick Davies, a highly regarded investigative journalist at British newspaper the *Guardian*, heard about Manning's leaked documents. To him, it sounded like the biggest story of the moment. He contacted Assange, urging him to release Manning's material to the world via his newspaper, and Assange eventually assented to a meeting. At a Belgian hotel in June 2010, Davies and his colleague Ian Traynor met the head of WikiLeaks. After hours of discussion, Assange suddenly handed over a napkin on which he'd circled some words and the hotel's logo, adding 'no spaces', and written the letters GPG – the encryption system used for the temporary website where he had uploaded the file.[328] The *Guardian* now had access to a quarter of a million secret diplomatic cables (see page 80).

ASSANGE'S BACK-UP PLAN

Julian Assange distrusted the mainstream media and was concerned about the safety of the leaked materials: 'I copied the 250,000 documents and stashed them first with contacts in Eastern Europe and Cambodia. I also put them on an encrypted laptop and had it delivered to [WikiLeaks supporter] Daniel Ellsberg, the hero of the Pentagon Papers [documents from an official report about the USA's role in the Vietnam War, leaked in 1971]... We also knew he could be trusted to publish the whole lot during a crisis.'[329]

Edward Snowden

'I'm willing to sacrifice [my former life] because I can't in good conscience allow the US government to destroy privacy, internet freedom and basic liberties for people around the world with this massive surveillance machine they're secretly building.'

Edward Snowden[330]

Former US National Security Agency (NSA) subcontractor Edward Snowden also knew exactly how to leak confidential information beneath the radar (see pages 75–7). In May 2013 he took leave from his job in Hawaii and flew to Hong Kong, beyond the reach of US law enforcement, taking encrypted access to thousands of secret NSA and British security service GCHQ documents.[331] Following in Assange's footsteps, he held clandestine meetings with journalists from the *Guardian*, which published a series of revelations over the summer.[332]

Snowden was also in contact with Berlin-based American film-maker Laura Poitras, who went on to make an Oscar-winning documentary about his story, *Citizenfour*. As Poitras says, 'If I wasn't already up to speed with using encryption, this leak might never have happened.'[333] Poitras had used the Darknet to communicate with WikiLeaks in the past. Snowden had contacted her using an anonymous email provider, reportedly Lavabit,[334] and the pair used encrypted communications. Poitras bought a laptop with cash and used it with the TAILS operating system: The Amnesic Incognito Live System. Installed with the Tor browser, TAILS boots from an exterior drive so that no trace of the operator's activities remain on the device after use. She used this laptop just for contacting Snowden and only in public places with Wi-Fi. Film footage was stored on encrypted drives. Until just before the premiere, Poitras showed the funders and distributors only small parts of her film. Throughout the process, Snowden remained nervous about security – he even put a blanket over his head and laptop when entering his pass phrase, just in case he was being covertly filmed.[335]

Despite the success of this cloak-and-dagger secrecy, in June 2013 Snowden outed himself as the source of the NSA revelations and became a wanted man, forced into exile from his homeland.

PAYING THE PRICE

• Chelsea (formerly Bradley) Manning was jailed in 2013 for 35 years. In January 2017, President Obama commuted her sentence to seven years (already served) and scheduled her release for May.

• Julian Assange: as of the end of 2016, he remained in his refuge at the Ecuadorian Embassy in London after refusing to be extradited to Sweden in 2012 to face rape allegations.[336]

• Edward Snowden: charged by the US with violating the Espionage Act, he was given asylum in Russia 2013 and would face prison if he returned home.[337]

PRIVACY FOR HUMAN RIGHTS

It's not just high-profile whistleblowers who can benefit from the anonymity of the Darknet. Human rights activists and dissidents in undemocratic countries risk life and limb when they express themselves online. Bloggers have been murdered

Demonstrators outside the White House, Washington, D.C., protesting in August 2013 against the sentencing of Chelsea (formerly Bradley) Manning to a lengthy jail term. The campaign was ultimately successful, and Chelsea Manning was scheduled for release in 2017..

in Bangladesh, flogged in Saudi Arabia and jailed in China and Iran. And anonymity is advantageous to those susceptible to surveillance in democratic nations.

Censorship in China

China is known for censoring the Internet for its citizens with the 'great firewall of China'; you can only use the Internet successfully via Chinese services such as Tencent or Baidu, and these are monitored by the authorities. Facebook is banned, and Apple News censored; if the Apple mobile operating system iOS detects a Chinese mobile signal, it replaces the news with the Chinese-approved version. If you use the Bing search engine, you will only see results that give a positive view of China. The government spies on Internet users, with dangerous consequences. In 2016, Zhang Haitao was sentenced to 19 years in prison for subversion for 69 WeChat and 205 Twitter posts in which he shared his views with sites such as Voice of America and Radio Free Asia – which the Chinese authorities deem 'foreign hostile websites'.[338]

To avoid censorship, using a VPN isn't sufficient because Chinese censors clamp down on such services. In response, some people are turning to Tor, although they probably use it mostly to evade censorship and access sites available on the surface web outside China rather than to access hidden sites on the Darknet.[339]

Iran: no Facebook freedom

Iranian blogger Soheil Arabi was arrested in November 2013 for Facebook posts that were said to be insulting to the Prophet. He was sentenced to death for blasphemy. Arabi was already in prison with a seven-and-a-half-year sentence for insulting the Supreme Leader Ayatollah Ali Khamenei. The blasphemy sentence was commuted to two years of studying theology – he was to study 13 religious books and use them to write an article about Islam. Iran has frequently cracked down on people openly voicing their criticism of religious institutions on Facebook.[340]

To avoid such a fate, the use of the Darknet browser Tor has spread within the activist community, assisted by digital rights group the Electronic Frontier Foundation. In summer 2009 Iranian dissident Nima Fatemi wanted to show the outside world that protests were erupting in Iran. He started using Tor and taught others how to implement the software. Now a technology expert and core member of the Tor project, Fatemi publicizes the browser among activists organizing against repressive regimes. In 2015, a video in several languages was released to educate people about Tor. It advised viewers: '[unwanted strangers] will see your real identity, precise location, operating system, all the sites you have visited, the browser you use to surf the web and so much more information about you and your life, which you probably didn't mean to share with unknown strangers who could easily use this data to exploit you. But not if you're using Tor.'[341]

The video used straightforward, non-technical language to make it accessible to a wide range of people. Nevertheless, there are quite a few things to understand to be able to run Tor properly so it's important for experts to share their knowledge.[342]

Library freedom in the United States

Even in democratic countries, certain minorities are particularly susceptible to surveillance and are turning to Tor. Alison Macrina founded the Library Freedom Project in the United States in July 2015. Libraries often serve poor and marginalized communities who don't have a computer at home, such as immigrants, the homeless and some Muslim Americans. Macrina travels around libraries in the United States, Canada and other countries to teach librarians about Tor and online privacy so they can advise library users and has hired Fatemi to run advanced training. In her experience '[Tor] really does protect and allow them to move in the online world unfettered from [sic] the pernicious effects of surveillance.'[343]

HOW TO BE ANONYMOUS

To use the Darknet, you need an anonymous browser; Tor is the best known. The urls on Tor are a meaningless string of letters and numbers with no indication of the site's content. The browser encrypts your IP address and routes it via other computers. You can use Tor on the surface Internet as well as on the Darknet. There's no censorship here and it is hard to control people's activities.[344]

THE ONION ROUTER – TOR

Usually a message is divided into packets of data, which are reassembled when they arrive. You can link the sender and receiver. To send messages anonymously via Tor, both sender and receiver must use this browser. They may also encrypt their messages as an extra precaution, for example with Pretty Good Privacy (PGP). If the message isn't encrypted, there's a possibility it will be seen when coming through the last Tor server, the exit node.[345] The message has several layers of encryption. It passes through a few nodes around the network. At each node, a layer of encryption is peeled off (like a layer of onion skin), which tells it to forward the message to the next node. This happens at each node until the message reaches its destination, where it will still have the original PGP encryption. Users can also set up hidden services, such as instant messaging, which are accessed via .onion domains.[346] The messages can't be seen if security services tap the servers.

Additional security features are continually being developed. The Dissent Project uses DC-nets – everyone sends their packets of information to everyone else. It's an anonymous way of broadcasting your message through blogging or micro-blogging, so perfect for expressing dissent. It's slow at the moment because of the large amounts of data being transferred, but speed will no doubt improve.[347]

Cryptophones

For conducting sensitive business with no risk of eavesdropping, why not buy a cryptophone? Based on the strongest encryption available, it can be used for mobile, satellite and landline calls from any location – even from a boat![348] In the United States, the algorithms for secure transmission by cryptophones are generally controlled by the NSA. There are different levels of security; Type 1 is for top-secret communications.[349]

Anonymous messaging

Social protest movements worldwide have used Twitter to spread their campaigns, but mass surveillance has made it dangerous; activists have been tracked down and arrested. A variety of alternatives to Twitter have emerged, including Twister, Jitsi and Jabber. Brazilian programmer Miguel Freitas invented Twister after hearing about the spy programs revealed by Snowden. It's a peer-to-peer microblogging system, powered by the users' own computers; because it is completely decentralized, no one can shut it down. No server keeps a record of the IP address you use to access Twister and it has end-to-end encryption, which means only the sender and receiver can read the message.[350] Because it's CPU intensive (it uses a lot of computer power) and slows down your machine, people volunteer to participate. In exchange, they can post adverts, called Promoted Posts. On Twister, you can follow people privately or publicly – which means you're visible to any Twister user but to no one outside the network.[351]

DARKNET SOCIAL
Want to chat on the Darknet? Darknet Social is a Tor-based social networking site, founded in mid-2015. Its dashboard is a public discussion board, where members' avatars and names appear when they post – others can like and comment as on the surface net.

Encrypting email

If you want to encrypt your email, you can use programs such as Mailpile, which allow you to create PGP keys in your email program to send encrypted messages.[352] There are no adverts here and you can rest assured your communications will remain private. Here's an example of an encrypted email, which requires a password to decrypt.[353]

```
Example Encrypted Text  Before                user clicks here
Hi world, I have a secret. Can you read it? Decrypt Encrypted Text [Toggle Visible]

#### Encrypted: decrypt with http://fourmilab.ch/javascrypt/
sdasldapqx123nasdfa09fafmzzxc02ksd3isfa94
#### End of encrypted message


Example Encrypted Text    After
Hi world, I have a secret. Can you read it? Hide Plaintext [Toggle Visible]

I like ice cream
```

Crypto-parties

'Ain't no party like a crypto apps install party'.

Australian privacy activist
Asher Wolf, 2012[354]

At the moment, it's assumed that if you encrypt your communications in a democracy, you must have something to hide. But the mass invasion of privacy has led to greater numbers turning towards encryption – people who simply don't want to be tracked, as well as whistleblowers and journalists protecting their sources. As Jamie Bartlett says, 'Most of us accept that, even in democracies, we need to be spied on sometimes – but that it should be limited, proportionate and not misused.'[355] Around the world, 'crypto-parties' are held to show people how to install encryption. At one crypto-party in Austin, Texas in 2015, the audience heard about VPNs, PGP and disk encryption.[356] People brought along their laptops to embark on their journey to private communications.

Icelandic privacy activist Smári McCarthy believes in encouraging everyone to use encryption to massively increase the cost of government surveillance. If they did, the cost would rise from 13 US cents a day (9p) to US $10,000 (more than £7,000). Then governments might restrict their spying to the few people they are really concerned about.[357] Alternatively, they might devote even greater resources to surveillance and even more people would transfer their communications to the Darknet.

**JACOB BERKSON,
MIGRANT SUPPORT ACTIVIST, UK**
'I've used Tor and PGP since the Snowden revelations. I thought it was outrageous that the government was spying on everyone. I thought I should take control of how I use my computer rather than accepting commercial email and web browsing. I spent half a day finding out about Tor, PGP and anti-tracking tools so that I could hide from mass surveillance. I realized I could use Jabber with Google chat to converse privately. It's a duty we have as citizens to do our bit to break mass surveillance.[358]

ISIS – A CASE STUDY IN DARKNET ANONYMITY

The horrifying terrorist attacks in Paris of November 2015 reignited the debate about privacy and surveillance. Mike Morell, former deputy director of the CIA, commented: 'We have in a sense had a public debate. That ... debate was defined by Edward Snowden ... and the concern about privacy. I think we're now going to have another debate about that. It's going to be defined by what happened in Paris.'[359]

In his book *Islamic State: The Digital Caliphate,* Abdel Bari Atwan explains how ISIS members and supporters have developed expertise in using the Darknet to avoid detection by their opponents. They use VPNs to conceal their IP addresses, particularly Ghost VPN, which works well with Tor for accessing the Darknet. For added security, ISIS members use TAILS, which the user can switch off instantly if necessary. They also use encrypted email services, such as bitmessage.ch; this system sends every encrypted email to hundreds of accounts, but only the intended recipient has the key to decrypt it. Even if the sender's account were being monitored, it would be impossible to deduce who was sending what to whom.

An anonymous bitmessage email account can be used to set up Facebook and Twitter accounts under an alias to send out extremist messages openly to large numbers of followers. Accounts are frequently closed down; between February and August 2016, Twitter suspended 235,000 accounts for promoting terrorism and threatening violence.[360] So ISIS organizers keep setting up new ones. Encrypted phones, known as 'Snowden phones', are popular with ISIS supporters because they can change numbers, making them extremely hard to trace, and are used with TAILS so no data is retained on the phone.[361]

COVERT CASH TRANSFER

ISIS members are expert users of cryptocurrencies for transferring funds. Using stored-value credit cards is popular. Here's how it works:

- The sender loads money on to a stored value card.

- They buy a prepaid disposable mobile with cash.

- They use an anonymous email account to register with a mobile payment service.

- They log on to make a payment, giving the number of the phone they want to send money to.

- The recipient receives the money on their disposable mobile and transfers it to their own stored value card, which they use to withdraw money from an ATM.

- Both people throw away the cards and mobiles.[362]

Immediately after the Paris attacks, it became clear that ISIS had organized them secretly on the Darknet. Within hours, the group posted a video there celebrating the terrorist strikes. Researcher Scot Terban found a new website by Al-Hayat Media Center that included nasheeds (songs about Islamic beliefs), poems for mujahideen and translations of statements claiming responsibility for attacks. It directed supporters to Telegram, an encrypted chat program commonly used by ISIS. Terban mirrored the site as incontrovertible proof of ISIS's activity on the Darknet.[363]

Given that the Paris attackers used encrypted communications on the Darknet, law enforcers want greater powers to be able to counter encryption, demanding backdoors to all software applications so they can access suspicious communications. But some have argued that this will not solve the problem. As IT journalist Steven Ragan comments, 'Encryption didn't cause the senseless, cowardly acts in Paris, evil human beings did ... Bulk record collection and weakened encryption will do nothing to stop terrorism.' There is a complex political background to the rise of ISIS in the Middle East and the growth of terrorism that cannot be solved at a technological level.[364]

'lhere is a more general debate about the extent to which Tor Hidden Services are used for criminal activity. Snowden's leaks showed how the NSA considers Tor a threat – even though it is partly funded by the US government. A confidential presentation from 2012 said: 'Tor stinks. We will never be able to de-anonymize all Tor users [but] we can de-anonymize a very small fraction.' Yet many activists say that cybercriminals form a small proportion of Tor users, and that growing numbers are adopting privacy tools because of worries about increasing surveillance. As Jamie Bartlett notes, 2–3 million people use Tor daily, mostly for legal activities. Even mainstream organizations are adopting it – Facebook has a Darknet site using .onion[365]. Musicians are exploring the Darknet in search of inspiration and excitement; in 2014, Aphex Twin released his album *Syro* on a Darknet site.[366] Artists like him, who are popular with their fan base although not widely known, can release music on this unusual platform and still do well. And legitimate Darknet activity is set to grow as more people seek to avail themselves of the liberty and anonymity it provides.

GROWING LESS OPAQUE?

Innovations for online privacy that started their life on the Darknet are gradually making their way into the mainstream and demonstrating their usefulness. Bitcoin is free of control by states or institutions and can be cheaper and more efficient than traditional money transfer. It has huge potential benefits for those without bank accounts and people sending remittances to their home country. Musicians have already started to see the advantages of cutting out the middleman. Blockchain is a distributed ledger, shared by all the participants and not controlled by any one party. Used to verify Bitcoin transactions, Blockchain could prove valuable for keeping government and property records and legal contracts; it could even permit people to avoid lawyers' fees.

The growth of mass surveillance has prompted privacy and human rights activists to develop the tools to evade it; this is of vital importance to those in undemocratic countries who want to communicate freely. Despite the clampdown on WikiLeaks and the high price paid by prominent whistleblowers such as Manning and Snowden, others continue to use Darknet cryptographic tools to leak confidential data without being traced by the authorities. Use of privacy tools is likely to grow, both in undemocratic countries and democracies that carry out mass surveillance, with education projects such as the Library Freedom Project in the United States teaching people how to use them.

The tools available for Darknet communications are continually developing, from improvements to Tor to anonymous messaging, encrypted emails and cryptophones. As well as increasing freedom for human rights activists, the technologies have been enthusiastically adopted by ISIS, which organizes terrorist actions on the Darknet. This has led to a debate about whether governments should be able to crack encryption when they deem it necessary, and the US government is working to do this. It seems that the balance is shifting away from individual rights to privacy and freedom towards greater surveillance. Mass surveillance is driving both legitimate human rights activities and illegal activity to the Darknet; the balance between them is unclear.

What is certain is that interest in this underground Internet world is growing and its use is expanding. The Darknet is widely publicized in articles, TV shows, films and high-profile court cases. More people are finding out about it, making it a less scary place. As futurist Thomas Frey notes, 'Far more Internet users are feeling it's safe to dip their toes in the dark waters.'[367] Search engines will gradually make the Darknet as easy to navigate as the surface web. Each time there's a flaw in security, hackers will come along to patch it up. According to Jamie Bartlett, the Darknet is going more mainstream and soon all social media companies and news outlets will have sites there: the 'Internet is about to get more interesting.'[368] If governments continue to extend mass surveillance, more people are likely to turn to the Darknet for both liberty and crime.

ACKNOWLEDGEMENT
OF KEY SOURCES

The author would like to acknowledge the following key sources for this book:

Julian Assange, *The Unauthorised Biography*, Edinburgh: Canongate Books Ltd, 2011

Julian Assange with Jacob Applebaum, Andy Müller-Maguhn, Jérémie Zimmermann, *Cypherpunks: Freedom and the Future of the Internet*, New York: OR Books, 2012

Abdel Bari Atwan, *Islamic State: The Digital Caliphate*, London: Saqi Books, 2015

Jamie Bartlett, *The Dark Net*, London: Windmill Books, 2015

Gabriella Coleman, *Hacker, Hoaxer, Whistleblower, Spy: The Many Faces of Anonymous*, London, New York: Verso, 2015

Misha Glenny, *Dark Market: Cyberthieves, Cybercops and You*, London: Bodley Head, 2011

David Leigh and Luke Harding, *WikiLeaks: Inside Julian Assange's War on Secrecy*, London: Guardian Books, 2011

Parmy Olson, *We Are Anonymous: Inside the Hacker world of LulzSec, Anonymous and the Global Cyber Insurgency*, London: William Heinemann, 2013

Thomas Rid, *Cyber War Will Not Take Place*, London: C. Hurst & Co, 2013

Daniel Sui, James Caverlee and Dakota Rudesill, *The Deep Web and the Darknet: A Look Inside the Internet's Massive Black Box*, Wilson Center, August 2015

Paul Vigna and Michael J. Casey, *Cryptocurrency: The Future of Money?* London: Vintage, 2016

NOTES

Disclaimer: The website references provided by the author are all current at the time of publication of this book.

1 http://www.theguardian.com/news/2016/apr/07/david-cameron-admits-he-profited-fathers-offshore-fund-panama-papers

2 Gabriella Coleman, *Hacker, Hoaxer, Whistleblower, Spy: The Many Faces of Anonymous*, London, New York: Verso, 2015, 260

3 http://www.wired.co.uk/news/archive/2013-05/30/online-aggression

4 http://www.wired.co.uk/news/archive/2015-11/16/cyberbullying-in-uk-schools

5 http://www.bullying.co.uk/cyberbullying/what-is-cyberbullying/

6 http://www.internetslang.com/SOOK-meaning-definition.asp

7 http://www.abc.net.au/news/2015-08-17/father-crusades-to-stop-cyber-bullies-after-daughters-suicide/6703668

8 http://www.heraldsun.com.au/news/victoria/grieving-parents-of-jessica-cleland-call-for-cyber-bullying-crackdown-after-their-daughter-was-bullied-to-death/news-story/40eb05d332b3c78834bd32e68dde1203

9 http://www.abc.net.au/7.30/content/2015/s4295135.htm

10 http://www.heraldsun.com.au/news/victoria/grieving-parents-of-jessica-cleland-call-for-cyber-bullying-crackdown-after-their-daughter-was-bullied-to-death/news-story/40eb05d332b3c78834bd32e68dde1203

11 http://www.abc.net.au/news/2015-08-17/father-crusades-to-stop-cyber-bullies-after-daughters-suicide/6703668

12 http://www.traynorseye.com/2012/09/meeting-troll.html

13 Jamie Bartlett, *The Dark Net*, London: Windmill Books, 2015, 35–40

14 Coleman, *op. cit.*, 20–29

15 http://www.redicecreations.com/radio/2015/09/RIR-150930.php

16 Bartlett, *op. cit.*, 39–40

17 http://www.dailydot.com/politics/dox-doxing-protection-how-to/

18 http://www.dailydot.com/opinion/gawker-donald-trump-dox-phone/

19 http://www.theguardian.com/technology/2014/oct/17/brianna-wu-gamergate-human-cost

20 http://patch.com/massachusetts/malden/what-is-doxing-yes-it-is-illegal

21 http://campbelllawobserver.com/doxing-a-legal-violation-of-privacy/

22 https://www.theguardian.com/society/2016/sep/08/online-grooming-of-children-often-alarmingly-fast-researchers-find

23 Bartlett, *op. cit.*, 122

24 https://www.nspcc.org.uk/fighting-for-childhood/news-opinion/online-grooming-cases-increase-50/

25 http://www.internetsafety101.org/Predatorstatistics.htm

26 http://www.europeanonlinegroomingproject.com/media/2076/european-online-grooming-project-final-report.pdf, 95

27 Bartlett, *op. cit.*, 125

28 *Ibid.*, 121

29 http://www5.austlii.edu.au/au/legis/cth/num_act/eosfca2015321/s3.html

30 http://www.telegraph.co.uk/news/worldnews/australiaandthepacific/newzealand/11725668/New-Zealand-makes-internet-trolling-illegal.html

31 http://www.smh.com.au/nsw/bega-teacher-arrested-for-attempting-to-groom-13yearold-girl-20150619-ghso59.html and http://www.abc.net.au/news/2015-06-19/nsw-catholic-school-teacher-charged-over-online-grooming-of-13yo/6559826

32 http://www.wired.co.uk/news/archive/2013-05/30/online-aggression

33 https://www.irjet.net/archives/V2/i2/Irjet-v2i2194.pdf

34 http://cybersecurityventures.com/cybersecurity-market-report/

35 C. Herley *IEEE Secur. Priv.* 12, 14–19; 2014

36 http://www.tomsguide.com/us/bad-passwords-data-breach,news-24005.html

37 https://blog.malwarebytes.org/fraud-scam/2014/08/email-hijack-leads-to-i-was-robbed-send-me-money-scam/

38 Anonymous source.

39 Michael Aaron Dennis, 'Cybercrime', Encyclopedia Britannica http://library.eb.co.uk/levels/adult/article/1623

40 For more on 419 scams, see: http://www.ieee-security.org/ TC/SPW2013/papers/data/5017a143.pdf

41 https://www.microsoft.com/security/pc-security/virus-whatis. aspx

42 http://study.com/academy/lesson/what-is-cyber-crime-definition-types-examples.html

43 http://www.cisco.com/c/en/us/about/security-center/virus-differences.html#5

44 https://www.microsoft.com/security/pc-security/spyware-whatis.aspx

45 http://us.norton.com/scareware

46 Misha Glenny, *Dark Market, Cyberthieves, Cybercops and You*, London: Bodley Head, 2011, 91

47 http://rp1.abs-cbnnews.com/business/09/18/15/inside-job-senior-citizen-loses-p159000-unauthorized-online-transfer

48 https://www.fightingidentitycrimes.com/case-study-tax-identity-theft/

49 Michael Aaron Dennis, 'Cybercrime', Encyclopedia Britannica http://library.eb.co.uk/levels/adult/article/1623

50 http://www.esecurityplanet.com/network-security/europes-data-protection-regs-what-you-need-to-know-1.html

51 http://www.zdnet.com/article/biometrics-the-password-you-cannot-change/

52 Spain: CNN MoneyTech, 26 July 2012 http://money.cnn. com/2012/07/26/technology/iris-hacking/index.htm?iid=EL

53 http://www.zdnet.com/article/biometrics-the-password-you-cannot-change/

54 http://inpressco.com/wp-content/uploads/2015/02/ Paper63352-354.pdf

55 http://www.reuters.com/article/us-usa-cyberattack-findikoglu-idUSKBN0P41XT20150624 and http://www. washingtontimes.com/news/2016/mar/2/ercan-findikoglu-turkish-computer-hacker-admits-ro/

56 http://www.nature.com.ezproxy.sussex.ac.uk/news/ cybercrime-fighters-target-human-error-1.16933

57 http://www.thisismoney.co.uk/money/saving/article-2955442/ Banks-hit-largest-cyber-crime-mercy-hackers.html and http://

www.kaspersky.com/about/news/virus/2015/Carbanak-cybergang-
steals-1-bn-USD-from-100-financial-institutions-worldwide

58   http://www.kaspersky.com/about/news/virus/2015/Carbanak-
cybergang-steals-1-bn-USD-from-100-financial-institutions-
worldwide

59   Misha Glenny, *op. cit.*, 41–48

60   *Ibid.*, 52

61   *Ibid.*, 55–56

62   https://nakedsecurity.sophos.com/2013/12/16/18-months-
for-supercomputer-hacker-18-years-for-carderplanet-boss/

63   Yahoo finance 26 Nov 2015

64   http://www.philb.com/fakesites.htm and http://www.philb.
com/fakesites2.htm

65   Michael Aaron Dennis, 'Cybercrime', Encyclopedia
Britannica http://library.eb.co.uk/levels/adult/article/1623

66   http://usa.chinadaily.com.cn/business/2015-11/03/
content_22354800.htm

67   http://www.usnews.com/news/business/articles/2016-12-21/
us-puts-alibaba-back-on-notorious-markets-blacklist/

68   http://www.phhttp://www.japantimes.co.jp/news/2015/09/02/
national/crime-legal/chiba-man-24-arrested-selling-bogus-autographed-
pop-idol-clothing-items/#.VouENNCFknUilb.com/fakesites.htm

69   http://www.csoonline.com/article/2978935/cyber-attacks-
espionage/cybercrime-by-wire-fraud-what-s-covered.html

70   http://www.cbsnews.com/news/whatsapp-users-get-played-
in-pump-and-dump-scheme/

71   '"Sonny Boy" and his ghost employees' by Annette
Simmons-Brown, *Fraud Magazine,* June 2015 http://www.fraud-
magazine.com/article.aspx?id=4294989126

72   http://uk.businessinsider.com/7-important-cybersecurity-
companies-2015-5?op=1

73   https://securityaffairs.co/wordpress/46186/breaking-news/
researchers-devised-recaptcha.html

74   http://www.nature.com.ezproxy.sussex.ac.uk/news/
cybercrime-fighters-target-human-error-1.16933

75   http://technical.ly/philly/2015/07/15/simply-secure-sara-
scout-sinclair-brody/

76   https://simplysecure.org/what-we-do/

77   https://www.hrw.org/news/2014/07/25/clear-eyed-look-mass-
surveillance

78 http://www.tamimi.com/en/magazine/law-update/section-11/
september-5/cyber-crimes-fighting-unlawful-immitation-and-
fraudulent-schemes.html

79 http://www.emirates247.com/news/emirates/uae-cybercrime-
law-immoral-video-2015-09-21-1.604258

80 http://www.thenational.ae/uae/courts/footballers-accused-of-
cyber-crime-in-abu-dhabi appeal sentence

81 http://www.coe.int/en/web/conventions/full-list/-/
conventions/treaty/185/signatures?p_auth=CvFVUble

82 https://cardnotpresent.com/report-online-fraud-biggest-
challenge-for-emea-companies-now-and-in-the-future-
july-23-2015/

83 http://www.kaspersky.com/about/news/virus/2015/Carbanak-
cybergang-steals-1-bn-USD-from-100-financial-institutions-
worldwide

84 http://www.japantoday.com/category/crime/view/stopping-
online-counterfeiters-a-big-challenge

85 Coleman, *op. cit.*, 171

86 http://arstechnica.com/uncategorized/2008/09/scientology-
fights-critics-with-4000-dmca-takedown-notices/

87 https://www.eff.org/wp/riaa-v-people-five-years-later

88 https://www.eff.org/issues/acta

89 Coleman, *op. cit.*, 346

90 http://searchnetworking.techtarget.com/definition/peer-to-
peer

91 Julian Assange with Jacob Applebaum, Andy Müller-
Maguhn, Jérémie Zimmermann, *Cypherpunks: Freedom and the
Future of the internet*, New York: OR Books, 2012, 81

92 http://www.fastcompany.com/3027441/the-infinite-lives-of-
bittorrent

93 Coleman, *op. cit.*, 111

94 *Ibid.*, 97

95 *Ibid.*, 100

96 http://www.theregister.co.uk/2010/09/28/acs_ico/

97 Coleman, *op. cit.*, 101

98 http://eur-lex.europa.eu/legal-content/EN/
TXT/?qid=1433409601658&uri=CELEX:52015DC0192

99 http://www.cbc.ca/news/politics/c-51-controversial-anti-
terrorism-bill-is-now-law-so-what-changes-1.3108608

100 Coleman, *op. cit.*, 408

101 http://anonhq.com/anonymous-attacks-canadian-government-opcyberprivacy/

102 https://anoninsiders.net/opcyberprivacy-ddosaftermath-3086/

103 Thomas Rid, *Cyber War Will Not Take Place*, London: C. Hurst & Co, 2013, 113–14

104 *Ibid.*, 120

105 *Ibid.*, 115

106 Coleman, *op. cit.*, 243–45

107 *Ibid.*, 243–45

108 *Ibid.*, 245

109 http://www.pcworld.com/article/216547/Sony_Sues_PS3_Hackers.html

110 http://wololo.net/2016/04/04/how-to-install-and-run-linux-on-your-ps4/

111 http://www.dailystar.co.uk/tech/news/471629/TalkTalk-cyber-attack-customer-details-stolen

112 http://uk.businessinsider.com/talktalk-80000-ransom-Bitcoin-krebs-2015-10

113 http://www.lbc.co.uk/exclusive-lbc-tracks-down-talk-talk-hacking-victims--119043

114 http://www.thisismoney.co.uk/money/markets/article-3361615/ TalkTalk-boss-Dido-Harding-refuses-say-sorry-customers-suffered-financial-losses-following-cyber-attack.html

115 http://www.itpro.co.uk/security/24136/talktalk-hack-what-to-do-if-hackers-have-your-data-17

116 https://www.theguardian.com/technology/2016/dec/14/yahoo-hack-security-of-one-billion-accounts-breached

117 http://arstechnica.com/security/2015/07/uk-man-accused-of-hacking-spree-on-uk-government-is-arrested-again/

118 http://www.theguardian.com/technology/2015/jul/16/british-man-lauri-love-accused-hacking-us-government-computer-networks-arrested

119 Parmy Olson, *We Are Anonymous: Inside the Hacker World of LulzSec, Anonymous and the Global Cyber Insurgency*, London: William Heinemann, 2013

120 *Ibid.*, 14

121 http://arstechnica.com/tech-policy/2011/02/virtually-face-to-

face-when-aaron-barr-met-anonymous/

122 Coleman, op. cit., 210

123 Olson, op. cit., 20

124 Olson, op. cit., 21

125 Coleman, op. cit., 284

126 http://www.globalpost.com/dispatches/globalpost-blogs/ the-grid/stratfor-hired-corporations-monitor-activists

127 Coleman, op. cit., 339

128 http://www.theguardian.com/technology/2013/nov/15/ jeremy-hammond-anonymous-hacker-sentenced

129 Coleman, op. cit., 379

130 Bartlett, op. cit., 99

131 http://blog.oup.com/2015/12/piracy-cybercrime-terrorism-security/

132 Coleman, op. cit., 303

133 https://www.finextra.com/newsarticle/25696/gchq-launched-ddos-attack-against-anonymous-members

134 http://deadspin.com/5972527/she-is-so-raped right now-former-student-jokes-about-the-steubenville-accuser-the-night-of-the-alleged-rape

135 http://www.motherjones.com/politics/2013/05/anonymous-rape-steubenville-rehtaeh-parsons-oprollredroll-opjustice4rehtaeh

136 Coleman, op. cit., 370

137 http://www.nytimes.com/2014/01/19/magazine/the-online-avengers.html?_r=0

138 Peter Preston, 'Julian Assange set a benchmark for freedom', the *Guardian,* 7 February 2016 http://www.theguardian.com/ media/2016/feb/07/julian-assange-benchmark-freedom-information-act

139 David Leigh and Luke Harding, *WikiLeaks: Inside Julian Assange's War on Secrecy,* London: Guardian Books, 2013, 66–67

140 *Julian Assange: The Unauthorised Biography*, Edinburgh: Canongate Books Ltd, 2011, 195

141 Rid, op. cit., 131

142 Parmy Olson, https://books.google.co.uk/books?id=uc E1AAAAQBAJ&pg=PT88&dq=parmy+olson+botnet&hl=en& sa=X&ved=0ahUKEwiI9uSwyI3LAhVIxRQKHZR2AqIQ6AEII zAB#v=onepage&q=parmy%20olson%20botnet&f=false, 122

143 Coleman, op. cit., 101–02

144 http://searchsecurity.techtarget.com/definition/botnet

145 Coleman, *op. cit.,* 127

146 *Ibid.,* 135

147 Rid, *op. cit.,* 132–33

148 Coleman, *op. cit.,* 192

149 *Ibid.,* 192

150 *Ibid.,* 149–50

151 *Ibid.,* 144

152 Olson, *op. cit.*

153 Coleman, *op. cit.,* 153

154 *Ibid.,* 166

155 *Ibid.,* 409

156 *Ibid.,* 199

157 http://news.trust.org//item/20131202221659-rcjtk

158 Coleman, *op. cit.,* 140–41

159 *Ibid.,* 384–85

160 *Ibid.,* 410–11

161 *Ibid.,*140–41

162 *Ibid.,* 140

163 *New York Times* – 'F.B.I. Informant Is Tied to Cyberattacks Abroad', cited in Coleman, 360

164 Coleman, *op. cit.,* 391

165 http://motherboard.vice.com/read/hacker-claims-responsibility-for-the-hit-on-hacking-team

166 http://www.techworld.com/picture-gallery/security/worlds-7-most-infamous-surveillance-spyware-programs-3620879/#2

167 http://www.techworld.com/picture-gallery/security/worlds-7-most-infamous-surveillance-spyware-programs-3620879/#1

168 http://www.securityweek.com/ukraine-power-outages-not-directly-caused-malware-experts

169 Rodrigo Bijou: 'Governments don't understand cyber warfare. We need hackers', TED Talks, June 2015 https://www.ted.com/talks/rodrigo_bijou_governments_don_t_understand_cyber_warfare_we_need_hackers?language=en

170 Rid, *op. cit.*

171 Rid, *op. cit.,* 84

172 Encyclopedia Britannica, Cybercrime, http://library.eb.co.uk/levels/adult/article/1623

173 Rid, *op. cit.,* 100

174 http://www.techworld.com/blog/war-on-error/duqu-attack-on-kaspersky-lab-is-assault-on-whole-security-industry-3615338/
175 http://www.computing.co.uk/ctg/news/2426296/russian-government-behind-seven-year-cyber-espionage-campaign-by-dukes-hacking-group
176 http://globalriskadvisors.com/state-sponsored-cyber-threats-iran/#blog
177 Rid, *op. cit.*, 94
178 https://www.washingtonpost.com/world/national-security/us-israel-developed-computer-virus-to-slow-iranian-nuclear-efforts-officials-say/2012/06/19/gJQA6xBPoV_story.html
179 http://cyberattacksquad.com/iranian-cyber-espionage-plot-against-israel-uncovered/
180 http://www.algemeiner.com/2015/11/09/us-israel-security-firm-reveals-global-cyber-espionage-operation/#
181 http://www.technologyreview.com/featuredstory/538201/cyber-espionage-nightmare/
182 David Talbot, *MIT Technology Review* http://www.technologyreview.com/featuredstory/538201/cyber-espionage-nightmare/
183 Rid, *op. cit.*, 32
184 *Ibid.*, 32–33
185 *Ibid.*, 43–46
186 *Ibid.*, 46
187 *Ibid.*, 53
188 *Ibid.*, 61–62
189 *Ibid.*, 56
190 *Ibid.*, 64
191 http://www.nytimes.com/2015/02/23/us/document-reveals-growth-of-cyberwarfare-between-the-us-and-iran.html?_r=0
192 Rid, *op. cit.*, 54
193 http://www.bbc.co.uk/news/world-europe-34818994
194 http://www.nytimes.com/2015/11/20/world/europe/paris-attacks.html
195 Abdel Bari Atwan, *Islamic State: The Digital Caliphate*, London: Saqi Books, 2015, ix
196 *Ibid.*, 16
197 *Ibid.*, x, 24
198 http://www.popsci.com/terror-on-twitter-how-isis-is-taking-

war-to-social-media

199   http://www.vox.com/2016/1/26/10830748/isis-video-paris

200   Atwan, *op. cit.*, 22

201   http://www.popsci.com/terror-on-twitter-how-isis-is-taking-war-to-social-media

202   Rid, *op. cit.*, 19

203   Atwan, *op. cit.*, 20–21

204   http://www.popsci.com/terror-on-twitter-how-isis-is-taking-war-to-social-media

205   Atwan, *op. cit.*, 20–21

206   http://www.salon.com/2016/01/17/turn_on_tune_in_defect_isis_is_now_broadcasting_a_satellite_tv_channel_in_iraq_partner/

207   Atwan, *op. cit.*, 125

208   http://blogs.csc.com/2016/02/04/breaking-down-the-threat-of-cyber-terrorism/

209   http://www.scmagazine.com/isis-hacking-group-migrating-to-threema/article/469537/

210   http://www.theguardian.com/world/2016/jan/13/ruqia-hassan-killed-for-telling-truth-about-isis-facebook and http://mtv.com.lb/news/english_highlights/556332/isis_jihadists_kill_journalist,_pose_as_her_on_social_media_to_entrap_others

211   Atwan, *op. cit.*, 30

212   http://time.com/4114182/anonymous-paris-attacks/

213   http://www.pinknews.co.uk/2016/06/16/hackers-hijack-isis-twitter-accounts-following-orlando-massacre/

214   Rid, *op. cit.*, 158–59

215   *Ibid.*, 104–05

216   http://www.ft.com/cms/s/0/0dbcab36-63be-11e5-a28b-50226830d644.html#axzz3x2NBoFB2

217   http://blogs.cfr.org/cyber/2016/09/28/the-u-s-china-cyber-espionage-deal-one-year-later/http://blogs.cfr.org/cyber/2016/09/28/the-u-s-china-cyber-espionage-deal-one-year-later/

218   Julian Borger, 'Trident is old technology: the brave new world of cyber warfare', in the *Guardian*, 16 January 2016

219   http://www.computing.co.uk/ctg/news/2426296/russian-government-behind-seven-year-cyber-espionage-campaign-by-dukes-hacking-group

220 https://ccdcoe.org/event/cyber-defence-exercises.html

221 Julian Borger, the *Guardian, op. cit.*

222 https://www.ted.com/talks/rodrigo_bijou_governmcnts_don_t_understand_cyber_warfare_we_need_hackers?language=en

223 http://www.technologyreview.com/featuredstory/538201/cyber-espionage-nightmare/

224 http://fortune.com/2016/03/23/apple-fbi-qa/ and http://www.cnet.com/news/the-apple-vs-fbi-drama-isnt-close-to-over-yet/ http://www.nytimes.com/2016/02/18/technology/explaining-apples-fight-with-the-fbi.html?_r=0

225 http://www.theguardian.com/uk-news/2015/jan/31/british-army-facebook-warriors-77th-brigade

226 http://edition.cnn.com/2015/01/28/europe/france-anti-radicalization-website/

227 Atwan, *op. cit.*, 31

228 Rid, *op. cit.*, 79 and http://www.cnet.com/news/hacker-says-he-broke-into-texas-water-plant-others/

229 https://www.youtube.com/watch?v=absaM9HliHw, 8 mins in

230 http://www.rollingstone.com/politics/news/the-battle-for-the-dark-net-20151022

231 http://www.rollingstone.com/politics/news/the-battle-for-the-dark-net-20151022

232 Daniel Sui, James Caverlee and Dakota Rudesill, *The Deep Web and the Darknet*, Wilson Center, October 2015, https://www.wilsoncenter.org/publication/the-deep-web-and-the-darknet

233 *Ibid.*

234 http://www.rollingstone.com/politics/news/the-battle-for-the-dark-net-20151022

235 Sui, Caverlee and Rudesill, *op. cit.*, 10

236 http://www.digitaltrends.com/computing/a-beginners-guide-to-tor-how-to-navigate-through-the-underground-internet/

237 https://www.torproject.org/docs/hidden-services.html.en

238 http://www.popsci.com/dark-web-revealed and https://www.deepdotweb.com/grams-search-darknet-marketplaces

239 http://www.huffingtonpost.com/2013/07/18/tor-snowden_n_3610370.html

240 http://www.popsci.com/dark-web-revealed

241 http://www.rollingstone.com/politics/news/the-battle-for-the-dark-net-20151022
242 http://www.dailydot.com/crime/dpr-silk-road-variety-jones/
243 https://www.youtube.com/watch?v=absaM9HliHw
244 Bartlett, *op. cit.*, 135
245 https://www.youtube.com/watch?v=absaM9HliHw
246 http://www.wired.com/2015/04/silk-road-1/ and http://www.wired.com/2015/05/silk-road-2/
247 Bartlett, *op. cit.,* 142
248 James Martin, http://theconversation.com/fair-trade-cocaine-and-conflict-free-opium-the-future-of-online-drug-marketing-30127
249 James Martin, *Drugs on the Darknet*, London: Palgrave, 2014, 39–40
250 Bartlett, *op. cit.,* 162
251 *Ibid.,* 148–49
252 Jamie Bartlett, https://www.ted.com/talks/jamie_bartlett_how_the_mysterious_dark_net_is_going_mainstream/transcript?language=en
253 Jamie Bartlett, http://www.telegraph.co.uk/technology/internet/11466413/What-dark-net-drug-buyers-say-about-their-dealers.html
254 Jamie Bartlett, https://www.ted.com/talks/jamie_bartlett_how_the_mysterious_dark_net_is_going_mainstream/transcript?language=en
255 Bartlett, *op. cit.,* 155
256 https://www.globaldrugsurvey.com/wp-content/uploads/2016/06/TASTER-KEY-FINDINGS-FROM-GDS2016.pdf
257 http://www.theguardian.com/society/datablog/2015/jun/08/global-drug-survey-2015-buy-online-darknet-silk-road
258 Bartlett, *op. cit.,* 162
259 Ross Whitaker, 'Why I had to buy my wife's inhaler on the Darknet', 14 July 2015 http://motherboard.vice.com/read/why-i-had-to-buy-my-wifes-inhaler-on-the-dark-web
260 Bartlett, *op. cit.,* 91–94
261 Akif Khan, 'Bitcoin – payment method or fraud prevention tool?' *Computer Fraud & Security*, Volume 2015, Issue 5, May 2015, 16–19
262 Bartlett, *op. cit.,* 94
263 http://www.coindesk.com/hyper-anonymising-Bitcoin-service-

dark-wallet-launches-today/

264 http://themerkle.com/news/dark-wallet-offers-privacy-and-anonymity-to-Bitcoin-uscrs/

265 http://blog.coinkite.com/post/97397052686/public-obelisk-server-for-the-community

266 http://themerkle.com/news/dark-wallet-offers-privacy-and-anonymity-to-Bitcoin-uscrs/

267 Bartlett, *op. cit.*, 106

268 Bartlett, http://www.brooklynrail.org/2015/07/books/sand-in-the-machine

269 http://krebsonsecurity.com/2013/11/no-bail-for-alleged-silk-road-mastermind/

270 http://www.wired.com/2015/04/silk-road-1/ and http://www.wired.com/2015/05/silk-road-2/

271 http://www.wired.com/2015/07/fbi-spent-775k-hacking-teams-spy-tools-since-2011/

272 http://upstart.bizjournals.com/entrepreneurs/hot-shots/2015/02/09/the-man-behind-darpa-s-search-engine-for-sex.html?page=all

273 http://www.rollingstone.com/politics/news/the-battle-for-the-dark-net-20151022

274 Sui, Caverlee and Rudesill, *op. cit.*

275 *Ibid.*

276 A guide for people involved with Anonymous: https://encyclopediadramatica.se/Rules_of_the_Internet

277 Marc Goodman, cited in Chris Campbell, 'Dark Net: The Most Disgusting LFT Episode Ever', Laissez Faire, https://lfb.org/dark-net-the-most-disgusting-lft-episode-ever/ Accessed 14 February 2017

278 Bartlett, *op. cit.*, 126–27

279 http://www.cybersalon.org/darknct/

280 Bartlett, *op. cit.*, 116–27

281 http://www.cracked.com/personal-experiences-1760-5-things-i-learned-infiltrating-deep-web-child-molesters.html

282 http://virtualglobaltaskforce.com/what-we-do/

283 Bartlett, *op. cit.*, 125

284 *Ibid.*, 126–27

285 https://www.iwf.org.uk/about-iwf/iwf-blog/post/417-harriet-lester---latest-technology-combating-child-sexual-abuse-images-

online-a-game-changer

286 *Ibid.*

287 http://motherboard.vice.com/read/the-fbis-unprecedented-hacking-campaign-targeted-over-a-thousand-computers

288 Sui, Caverlee and Rudesill, *op. cit.,* 10

289 http://motherboard.vice.com/read/the-fbis-unprecedented-hacking-campaign-targeted-over-a-thousand-computers

290 Julian Assange et.al., *Cypherpunks: Freedom and the Future of the internet,* op. cit., 133–34

291 Paul Vigna and Michael J. Casey, *Cryptocurrency: The Future of Money?* London: Vintage, 2016, 1–3

292 Bartlett, *op. cit.*, 5

293 Khan, *op. cit.,* 16–19

294 Bartlett, *op. cit.,* 90

295 Vigna and Casey, *op. cit.,* 190

296 https://news.bitcoin.com/kenya-bank-m-pesa-legislation/ and https://www.bitpesa.co

297 https://www.bitpesa.co/blog/connecting-payments-with-africa-and-china/

298 Vigna and Casey, op. cit., 190–91

299 http://bravenewcoin.com/news/musicians-turn-to-Bitcoin-why-didnt-we-hear-about-this-before/

300 http://www.coindesk.com/information/what-is-Bitcoin/

301 http://bravenewcoin.com/news/musicians-turn-to-Bitcoin-why-didnt-we-hear-about-this-before/

302 http://www.soundclick.com/bands/default.cfm?bandID=1302880

303 https://www.reddit.com/r/Bitcoin/comments/3yhtd0/just_released_my_first_single_after_14_years_of/

304 The hash function is important in cryptography. It takes an input of an arbitrary length and reduces it to a fixed length, e.g. 160 bits. https://cseweb.ucsd.edu/~mihir/cse207/w-hash.pdf

305 https://.org/en/how-it-works

306 https://www.ethereum.org

307 Akif Khan, *op. cit.*

308 Radio 4 Today programme, 19 January 2016

309 https://coincenter.org/link/the-uk-s-new-blockchain-welfare-benefits-trial-has-privacy-advocates-freaking-out

310 http://www.futuristspeaker.com/2015/09/the-future-of-the-darknet-9-critically-important-predictions/

311 Vigna and Casey, *op. cit.*, 225–6

312 http://cointelegraph.com/news/muse-blockchain-music-platform

313 Rid, *op. cit.*, 100

314 http://thenextweb.com/eu/2016/01/09/germany-reportedly-resumes-domestic-surveillance-efforts-with-the-nsa/#gref

315 Cybersalon, January 2015, The Future of the Dark Net, http://www.cybersalon.org/darknet/

316 http://www.wired.co.uk/news/archive/2015-01/13/david-cameron-hates-your-privacy

317 Julian Assange, *op. cit.*, 243

318 Leigh and Harding, *op. cit.*, 31

319 *Ibid.*, 21–22 and 29–30

320 *Ibid.*, 86

321 http://www.theguardian.com/world/blog/2009/nov/25/september-11-wikileaks-pager-messages

322 http://www.webopedia.com/TERM/V/VPN.html

323 Leigh and Harding, *op. cit.*, 51

324 *Ibid.*, 52

325 https://wikileaks.org/wiki/WikiLeaks:Submissions

326 Leigh and Harding, *op. cit.*, 75–76

327 *Ibid.*, 81

328 *Ibid.*, 90–91

329 Assange, op. cit., 244–45

330 http://www.theguardian.com/world/2013/jun/09/edward-snowden-nsa-whistleblower-surveillance

331 Leigh and Harding, *op. cit.*, 280

332 http://www.biography.com/people/edward-snowden-21262897#government-work

333 http://www.wired.com/2014/10/laura-poitras-crypto-tools-made-snowden-film-possible/

334 http://www.zdnet.com/article/dark-mail-debut-to-open-door-for-lavabit-return-ladar-levison/

335 http://www.wired.com/2014/10/laura-poitras-crypto-tools-made-snowden-film-possible/

336 http://www.theguardian.com/media/2016/jan/15/julian-assange-allowed-questioned-swedish-prosecutors-london

337 http://www.biography.com/people/edward-snowden-21262897#aftermath

338 http://chinachange.org/2016/02/21/appeal-begins-of-harsh-19-year-prison-term-given-xinjiang-based-activist-zhang-haitao/

339 http://motherboard.vice.com/read/what-firewall-chinas-fledgling-deep-web-community

340 http://www.theguardian.com/world/2015/sep/30/iran-death-sentence-commuted-theology-study

341 http://www.betaboston.com/news/2015/03/18/in-an-effort-to-educate-users-tor-animates-online-privacy/

342 https://www.torproject.org/download/download-easy.html.en#warning

343 https://blog.torproject.org/blog/what-tor-supporter-looks-alison-macrina

344 Jamie Bartlett, http://www.ted.com/talks/jamie_bartlett_how_the_mysterious_dark_net_is_going_mainstream

345 Leigh and Harding, *op. cit.,* 54–55

346 *Ibid.,* 53–54

347 http://motherboard.vice.com/read/dissent-a-new-type-of-security-tool-could-markedly-improve-online-anonymity

348 http://www.cryptophone.de

349 http://www.cryptomuseum.com/crypto/phone.htm

350 http://twister.net.co

351 http://www.socialmediaalternatives.org/archive/collections/show/12

352 https://www.howtoforge.com/tutorial/how-to-install-mailpile-with-nginx-on-ubuntu-15-10/

353 Dokucrypt: http://www.brickies.net/wiki/dokucrypt:start

354 Bartlett, *op. cit.,* 100

355 *Ibid.,* 102

356 https://www.alienvault.com/blogs/security-essentials/cryptoparty-at-austin-owasp

357 Bartlett, *op. cit.,* 98

358 Interview with author, Brighton, UK, January 2016

359 http://www.csoonline.com/article/3004648/security-awareness/after-paris-isis-moves-propaganda-machine-to-darknet.html

360 https://www.theguardian.com/technology/2016/aug/18/twitter-suspends-accounts-terrorism-links-isis

361 Atwan, *op. cit.*, 26

362 *Ibid.*, 26

363 http://www.csoonline.com/article/3004648/security-awareness/after-paris-isis-moves-propaganda-machine-to-darknet.html

364 http://www.csoonline.com/article/3004648/security-awareness/after-paris-isis-moves-propaganda-machine-to-darknet.html

365 Jamie Bartlett, https.//www.ted.com/talks/jamie_bartlett_how_the_mysterious_dark_net_is_going_mainstream/transcript?language=en

366 http://www.theguardian.com/music/2014/sep/23/musicians-embrace-darknet-uncensored-internet-web-surveillance

367 http://www.futuristspeaker.com/2015/09/the-future-of-the-darknet-9-critically-important-predictions/

368 https://www.ted.com/talks/jamie_bartlett_how_the_mysterious_dark_net_is_going_mainstream/transcript?language=en

INDEX